LAST NIGHT MY BED A BOAT OF WHISKEY GOING DOWN

LAST NIGHT MY BED A BOAT OF WHISKEY GOING DOWN

a novel in essays

Thomas E. Kennedy

new american press
Fort Collins, Colo.

new american press

© 2010 by Thomas E. Kennedy

All rights reserved. No part of this publication may be reproduced, stored in a retrieval system, or transmitted, in any form or by any means, electronic, mechanical, photocopying, recording, or otherwise, without the prior written permission of the copyright holder.

Printed in the United States of America

ISBN 978-0-9817802-8-3

For ordering information, please contact:

Ingram Book Group
One Ingram Blvd.
La Vergne, TN 37086
(800) 937-8000
orders@ingrambook.com

For media and review requests, please contact:

New American Press
Sales and Marketing Director
newamericanpress@gmail.com

Acknowledgements

"I Am Joe's Prostate" was first published in *New Letters* (2007), won a National Magazine Award for best essay in 2008, was reprinted in *Best American Magazine Writing 2008* and, in Danish translation, in *Euroman* and *The PEN anthology of Danish writers in other languages (Herfra min verden går, 2009, Ed. Anders Jerichow, Dina Yafasova, Mille Rode)*.

"Adventures of an Old Dude" first appeared in *New Letters (2010)*.

"Maybe Baby" was first runner up in the *Chautauqua* Fiction Competition (2010).

"Old Dude in the Free State" appeared in the inaugural issue of *Serving House: A Journal of Literary Arts*, April 2010 (www.ServingHouseJournal.com).

The excerpts from R. M. Rilke's poetry that appear in this book were translated by Stephen Mitchell.

This is a novel of creative nonfiction, a progress in short narratives. Characters and situations are not transcribed from life and resemblances are coincidental.

TABLE OF CONTENTS

Maybe Baby   13

Song of Experience   27

That Night on the Farm   40

In Turku It Is Snowing   49

I Am Joe's Prostate   58

Adventures of an Old Dude   74

Your Relationship Is Going Through Bad Weather   114

Last Night My Bed a Boat of Whiskey Going Down   130

Old Dude in the Free State   142

I Am a Slave to the Nudity of Women   151

For Daniel and Isabel, Søren and Leo

For Bob Stewart, David Bowen and Okla Elliott

*With thanks to Steve Davenport for the title
and to Ellen Akins, Walter Cummins, Duff Brenna,
and Barry Brent for help and encouragement*

To the Signora for her kiss

*And to all the old dudes everywhere
who refuse to go toes up just yet*

"I do not know with what resolve
I could stand against it, a naked woman
Asking of me anything."

        Alberto Ríos
        Teodoro Luna's Two Kisses

MAYBE BABY

The year is 1958. It is summer, three months since you turned fourteen, three weeks since you completed freshman year at Bishop Loughlin boy's high school, and three days since Antonia Giangrande, the sister of your friend Joey, told you that Beatriz Gomez de Gomez likes you. Now, with your friends Joey and Pancho following, your polished Flagg Brothers shoes lead you with purposeful strides to the St. Batholomew's School girls annex where Beatriz Gomez de Gomez is in eighth grade. You intend to kiss Beatriz Gomez de Gomez. And because Joey and Pancho are aware of your intention, you will have to do it. And you are frightened.

She is there on the play street outside the school. It is recess. She is wearing her school uniform, pleated grey skirt, white knee socks, white blouse with a maroon SBS embroidered on the pocket of the swelling front. Her face is part Indian, almond eyes, one of which is now squinted against the sun as she smiles at you. She has dimples. Your mouth is dry. She stands alone. Now is your chance. Then Bobby Anne Hague steps up and begins to speak to Beatriz, but Beatriz's eyes are still on you.

"You gonna do it?" Pancho urges.

"Shut up," you snap out the side of your mouth and step up to her, pinch the loose material of the sleeve of her blouse and tug a little. She follows you to the shelter of a tree.

You say, "Hi."

She says, "Hi?"

You clear your throat, say, "Some of us are going over to Joey and Antonia's. Would you like to come? With me?"

Still smiling, still squinting one eye against the June sunlight, she says, "I would like to. With you." But she has to go home first after school. She will meet you at four. This is unbearable. You want to kiss her as quickly as possible in order to end the agony of your fear of doing so. But she touches your arm – your *bare* arm – *she touches your bare arm!* – and then for a second she lays the warm palm of one hand against your chest. It feels so good. Then she takes it away. The school bell is ringing end of recess. A nun in black robes and veil, her face framed in starched white, stares at you with small dark eyes from the doorway of the red brick school building. Beatriz starts toward the nun, looks back once, smiles.

Now you can not run. Shame would follow you forever. Because then you would have to start hanging around in another neighborhood, make all new friends, but who would want to be your friend, a boy who ran from a kiss? You do not want to run. You want this. More than anything else in your life you want this.

You wait in Joey's half-dark living room for the minutes to pass until four, for Beatriz to arrive. A 45 plays on repeat on Joey's Webcor, Buddy Holly & the Crickets singing "Maybe Baby." Your stomach is queasy. Your left eye twitches. You look at your hand and see the trembling of your fingers. There is no exit. Antonia and Pancho and Joey sit eating from a fruit bowl in the dining area. You watch Joey select a fat peach, his thick black curls, black sideburns, full lips; Pancho, leanly muscular, his upper and lower teeth flashing in a Joker smile. There is a painting on the wall of a bare-breasted African woman. Pancho once sniggered at this painting, and Joey's mother said indignantly, "That's *art*!" You sit on the two-person sofa in the corner. Antonia, who is thin and dark with a wisp of dark fuzz on her upper lip, watches you with compassion. Joey is slurping juice from the peach, and Pancho is telling stupid jokes that he learned from his older brother Victor, so-called "Pierre" jokes. He does not understand that this is not a sexual moment. This is a moment of beauty unlike any you have ever experienced in all your fourteen years, something you have always wanted. You have always wanted to kiss a girl. You admit that freely to yourself now. Even when you were a little kid, forever, always, incessantly, you wanted to kiss a girl. More than anything you wanted to kiss a girl, but you never guessed how afraid you would be. Your older brother tells you stories about how he drives home from Rockaway Beach through Cross Bay in his '50 Ford convertible while some bimbo nibbles his ear and jazz plays on his car radio, and he is so cool. You realize abruptly that you are *not* cool. You are scared, and Beatriz is so beautiful with her high cheekbones and almond eyes and white smiling teeth and dimpled cheeks, her round hips and narrow waist and the sweetness of her knees showing between her pleated skirt and knee socks and her...breasts. That is the word. Breasts. Not the other word – she deserves better than that.

And oh god now the doorbell buzzes, and it could only be Beatriz, and you are not ready, you are such a punk, such an uncool punk with your Buddy Holly glasses and hair that keeps collapsing, but Antonia opens the door, and it is Beatriz, wearing a pink, open-throated blouse, so sheer you can see she wears a blue bra, her legs bare in white shorts, tight between her thighs so you get dizzy she is so beautiful. You rise to your feet and start to hold out your hand to her but it is shaking so you only gesture to the seat beside you on the sofa, and she comes right over to you. She has made a deal and she is keeping it. She takes your half out-stretched hand, and the two of you sit and look into one another's eyes.

She says, "Can I see you without your glasses?"

You know that people who wear glasses look weird when they take them off, but you see no way around this. You take them off, fold them, put them on the coffee table and look at her.

She says, "You're cute without your glasses." You feel your mouth sag, and she adds, "I mean, you're cute with them, too," and you remember that she told Antonia that she liked you before she ever saw you without your glasses. The blood is pounding in your ears, and you think, Well? Go on. And by god you kiss her. Just like that! You kiss her. On the mouth. Slowly, softly. Now you are glad your glasses are off, as you slide your lips across her cheek and fold your arms around her, palms flat against her warm back, and she leans into you, her body fits so wonderfully against yours, and you kiss the soft place where her neck meets her shoulder, kiss under her chin and alongside her nose, then one by one you kiss her hands, the backs and then the soft yielding cups of her palms. You close your eyes and are so happy and Buddy is singing "Maybe Baby," and goddamn, now *she* is kissing *your* neck and squeezing your hand tight as if she needs to cling to you, and then her fingers find the back of your head, and her fingernails are playing in the short hair there, and you dare to put your fingers underneath the long black drape of her hair, secret place where it curtains the nape of her silken neck, and you kiss her and you kiss her and Buddy sings "Maybe Baby."

The world changes then. Everything has become different. She whispers to you that she has to be home to help with dinner, but tomorrow is Saturday and she tells you she is free, and you ask if she would like to go with you to Rockaway Beach, and she says yes. She will meet you at the Woodside bus stop at ten. She turns away to go, but then turns back and looks at your face as though she wants to memorize it, she is looking everywhere on your face so you can feel her eyes seeing you. She reaches to the coffee table for your glasses, opens them carefully and slips them onto your face. Her palms bracket your checks as she kisses you once more and then is gone.

Antonia walks her home. Joey and Pancho, who at some point disappeared, re-emerge from the back room, and you can see that Joey looks differently at you now – with respect and envy but also the pleasure a friend feels for the good fortune of a friend. Pancho grins with his big white Joker teeth and cackles. "So, did Pierre behave himself, or what? *Down*, Pierre! *Down!*" You look at him with disdain. He is hopeless.

At Rockaway, Beach 98, you flap a white sheet out on the blazing white sand. Beatriz has brought sandwiches and a thermos of lemonade and paper cups and napkins, and you quickly strip to your swimsuit and flop onto your belly as she lifts her orange beach kimono over her head. The wonder of what you see as the kimono comes up and off convinces you that you will never be able to stand up again; you are trapped flat on your belly, the hot sand burning through the white sheet, and your agony makes you grateful that you have chosen the swim suit you chose, one that holds things down in place.

The day proceeds with a continual escalation of ecstasy. You kiss her in the water, bobbing in the waves, your fingers interlaced. You kiss her under the water, the two of you swimming toward one another, eyes opened, closed smiling lips meeting. You kiss the sea salt from her lips. You kiss her brown shoulders and her hands. You kiss her under the boardwalk where the sand is cool, the light muted. You kiss her behind a support post, her back leaned up against it, and your bodies press and rub together, and you realize that she could only have noticed the solidity of your consternation, but her eyes seem to tell you it is okay, she understands. She *understands!*

Afterwards, in the amusement park, you eat corn on the cob, salted and peppered and dripping with melted butter, and you kiss butter and salt from her lips and lead her by the hand into a photo booth – four pictures for a quarter – all four the same, the two of you with your mouths locked together, tongues touching, fingers in hair. You wait together impatiently by the booth for the strip of photos to fall out of the chute, Beatriz leaning against you, her shoulder beneath your arm, her hip against your…consternation…her dimples as she looks up into your eyes, and you don't care how long it takes for the photos to be developed, you just want to be here with her, anywhere with her.

The photos plop out then, and you smile at one another as you study them, looking from the pictures to one another's eyes, marveling at this photographic record of this amazing thing that is happening between you and her.

You tear the photo strip across the center – two pictures for her, two for you.

Your first mistake. Evidence.

Next morning your mother wakes you for Mass – which for once in your life will be a pleasure, you and Beatriz are going to Mass together, to sit side by side in the pew. You remember a movie you saw with Troy Donahue and Connie Stevens in which he kisses her in church and says, "I will kiss you in the house of God!" Your mother sees the pictures that you carelessly left out on your bureau and asks, in her most skeptical tone, "What is *this*?"

You remember suddenly the time when you were eight and she caught you and Joannie Teofilo in the basement, Joanie's shorts and underpants around her ankles as she allowed you to behold the beauty of the essence of girl, and your mother said, "Go upstairs, son. Joannie has to go home now." Joanie left crying, and your mother, washing dishes in the kitchen, her back to you, said, "It's all right this time because you didn't know any better. But don't ever do that again."

You told her you were sorry, but you *knew*, you *knew* you would do it again at any and every chance you ever got. You just never got another chance. Until now. And this time you will take a stand.

Your mother asks, "Is this your friend Beatriz? She's Latin American, isn't she? You'd better be careful, son, in that culture sometimes a kiss is as good as a marriage proposal."

And so what? you think. Then I could do what's described in that book you showed me about the Sacred Act of Motherhood and Fatherhood for Catholic Boys & Girls. Where the sacred organs of motherhood are joined with the sacred organs of fatherhood in order for the sacred seed to find the sacred womb and create sacred new life.

You would be happy to do that with Beatriz!

———

You are late for Mass. You sponge yourself, brush your teeth, Brylcream your pompadour, pull on black chinos and black T-shirt and your polished black leather Flagg Brothers shoes, comb your hair again, and hightail it across Elmhurst to the church. You haven't missed the first principal part of the Mass yet, and you stand by the holy water font and survey the crowded pews of the eleven o'clock, your skin pleasantly sun-burned and your mind aswim with memories of Beatriz's salt kisses. But where is she? You look and look, scanning pew after pew. No Beatriz.

Then someone comes up alongside you. Antonia. She signals with her eyes for you to step outside, and there on the top step of the broad concrete stairway leading down to Justice Avenue, she reports the terrible news: Señor Gomez de Gomez has found the pictures and has sent Beatriz away for the rest of the summer. In September, she will be entering a convent school in Dobb's Ferry.

Frantic, you demand, "But where is she now?"

Antonia looks at your mouth. You know that Antonia likes you, but she is your friend's sister. Out of the question. Besides, she is not your type, she is not Beatriz. "No one knows," she says. "When I saw her this morning, she didn't even know where she was being sent."

"You *saw* her!"

"She gave me this for you," Antonia says and hands you a small, fat envelope on which is written your name and upon your name an imprint of Beatriz's pink lipsticked mouth. With trembling fingers, you open the envelope to find not a letter, but a steel ID bracelet on which is engraved BEATRIZ.

Antonia says, "It's a girl's bracelet but she said there was no time for anything else and she wanted you to have something to remember her by."

You slip it over your hand and click shut the clasp, watch as it slides down your wrist towards your sunburned hand, stopped by the thickening bone. You look to Antonia's thin face, her brown eyes, her large mouth, the fuzz above her full lips. You stand with your arms by your sides as she hugs you tightly.

She says, "I'm sorry," but you just slouch down the stairway to the avenue, skip the rest of the Mass, walk home through the summer morning, wearing the ID bracelet with fierce pride although you feel the source of your pride is fragile as an egg. At home, you climb the stairs, shut yourself into your little room, turn on your Motorola radio, twist the dial to 1010 WINS New York, the AM rock and roll station. You bunch the pillow behind you, punching it hard, fold your arms beneath your head, lie there distantly hearing Jerry Lee Lewis, Chuck Berry, Fats Domino, Elvis, the Fleetwoods doing "Come Softly." Then Buddy Holly comes on with "Maybe Baby," and tears sting your eyes.

There is a tap on the door.

"Don't come in!" you shout.

Footsteps recede along the hall runner. You want to die. Every foul word you know slips in a furious whisper through your teeth. The anger is salvation. Preserve this saving fury, you think and punch your mattress, punch it again. Then your eyes fill again and this time you cry. You crumple up against your bedspread and hear the strange high sounds coming from your throat.

The anger is better. You seek to nourish it with thoughts of Señor Gomez de Gomez. You know that he is a diplomat who works at the UN. You picture yourself taking the IRT Flushing line into Manhattan, to Grand Central Station, striding from 42nd Street down to East 34th, marching up to the reception desk of the UN Secretariat Building, demanding to see Señor Gomez de Gomez, demanding... No. No demands. No. Just stating your case. Señor: I come from a good Catholic family. Señor, I have nothing but the highest respect for your daughter.

Respect! he thunders back at you. You call to take such a photograph of her, her, *defilement* respect! No, my boy, no no no, you will never to see my daughter again. Not for one hour. Not for one minute. *Never*!

You beg: Please, Señor. Please!

Dozing, you dream troubled dreams too strange to remember. When you wake it is dark. You hear the television set from downstairs. *Perry Mason* theme music. The air in the little room is humid, close. You are sweating. A mosquito whines at your ear. Your radio still plays softly. You hear steps on the hall runner again. A tap at the door.

"Go away!" you shout.

The steps recede. Is she in on this? Did she tell Beatriz's father about the photos? You look at the bracelet on your wrist, trace your fingertip delicately over the engraved letters there: B-E-A-T-R-I-Z.

Alan Freed is talking rapidly on the radio, inviting listeners to call in with requests and dedications. Then he is saying words that you hardly dare believe you are hearing: *And this one is for Tom Kennedy in Queens from Beatriz in Coney Island – Little Anthony*

& the Imperials with their big one: "Tears on My Pillow"!

Coney Island! She's in Coney Island! You hop out of bed, hurry up the hall to your parent's room where there is a telephone extension and you can call in private, without everyone downstairs listening. You dial Joey's number, get Antonia on the line. "She's in Coney Island. I just heard…"

"I heard, too!" she says. "Let me make some inquiries."

You shout down the stairway, "No one use the phone, okay?! I'm waiting for a very important call!"

You sit in the rocking chair in your parent's room in the dark, gazing out the screened windows at the leafy summer trees outside, waiting for the phone to ring. The trees are different now, too – trees you have seen all your life, all of your fourteen summers. Everything is different. You think about what Antonia said – "Let me make some inquiries." The sound of it gave you hope; it sounded like she knew what she was doing. Your fate is in her hands. You wait. You wait. You have to pee. You hold it. Then you can't hold it anymore, and you run down the hall to the bathroom, start to pee and hear the telephone ring. You whimper, try to stop peeing, but you can't. Your mother hollers up the stairs, "It's for you, Tom! A *girl*!"

Then you are lifting the receiver of the extension in your parent's room, holler down, "Hang up down there, okay?" You hear the click on the line, and Antonia is telling you, "She has a cousin on Neptune Avenue in Coney Island. I got the number and called. She'll meet you outside the Steeple Chase tomorrow at noon."

From Broadway in Elmhurst to Stillwell Avenue in Coney Island is a long subway ride, through three boroughs. You have to leave Long Island, crossing the East River from Queens onto Manhattan Island, ride down through Manhattan, re-cross the East River to Long Island, now into Brooklyn, and continue southwest to the foot of the island. It is muggy in the subway car, and by the time you are entering Brooklyn, you have been on the train for over an hour and have lost count of stops. This area of Brooklyn is less familiar to you than where your high school is. For a while there are mostly white faces on the subway, then mostly black, then mostly brown, then there are men and boys in heavy black clothes, black coils of hair hanging from beneath the brims of their black hats.

Then you are above ground again, and the train windows are open, and you can smell the iodine smell of the sea. The elevated train screeches around a sharp curve, and you cross water again, and you look out the opposite window and see the Cyclone roller coaster, high and looping and dirty white, and the tall erector-set structure of the Parachute Jump jutting up 250 feet over the Coney Island boardwalk.

You leave the train, wading into humid heat, sweating as you step along sandy Surf Avenue, a rolled towel tucked beneath your arm, toward the grinning toothy clown face medallion of Steeplechase Park. You are half an hour early, and you haven't eaten breakfast, so for fifteen cents you buy a foot-long hotdog at Nathan's with mustard and relish, and you don't know what is going to happen, but it is only June, the summer lies before you like an eternal green span. You wait outside the Steeplechase gates, beneath the painted wooden horses that circle around on a rail outside the top of the building, and you wonder if Señor Gomez de Gomez is going to force Beatriz to become a nun and whether that is legal, but then you think that he might make her go back to Colombia, and you don't even quite know where Colombia is except that it is very far away across water and mountains and jungle, and you get a leaden feeling inside your stomach that Beatriz might be taken from you. Once again, you tenderly trace your fingertip over the engraved letters of her name in the ID bracelet, and you wish that you had brought a present for her, maybe an ankle bracelet or a heart on a chain. You will bring one tomorrow. You will come every day to see her if she will let you. The whole summer is before you, and things can change by September. Maybe you will meet her family, maybe they will like you.

Then, from behind, hands cover your eyeglasses and her sweet voice says, "Guess who?" You spin, arms opened to encircle her, ready to kiss her mouth because you feel you have the right now, but you see that she is not alone. Antonia is with her. Your confusion must show on your face for the two girls giggle happily, and each loops an arm in one of yours, and they steer you toward the boardwalk.

Antonia spreads a blanket on the sand, and the three of you strip to your swimsuits and charge into the water. You dive into a wave, bob up and seize Beatriz to kiss her, but she twists away and swims around behind you and circles your arms tightly with hers. She is strong, and as you try to break her grip, Antonia surfaces in front of you, looks into your face and kisses you on the mouth. You laugh and swim away, still feeling her fuzz against your lip, trying to understand what is happening, but the two of them attack you in a splash fight, and you surrender to the fun.

Cooled down, you collapse on the blanket, a girl on either side of you, your laughter calming to a sleepy stillness. You turn your eyes to Beatriz. The side of her face against the blanket, she is watching you, one eye squinted shut above her dimpled smile. You reach your head forward and kiss her salty lips, and she kisses you back, but something has changed. It is not as it was before. After a moment, she draws back and says quietly, "Now kiss Antonia, too."

You shake your head.

"She'll feel left out," Beatriz whispers, and you whisper into her ear, "I can't just kiss anyone. I only want to kiss you."

She smiles, watching you with her almond Indian eyes, then shrugs and says, "Time for my nap," and turns her back. Things seem to be changing faster than you can follow; the moment of your certainty has vanished, and you no longer know what to do or say.

You put your hands behind your head and close your eyes and feel the sunlight tingling across the surface of your skin as you drift away from the order of your conscious perceptions into a place that is half beach, half train looping around a sharp curve into a tunnel that is a smiling clown mouth.

Abruptly you wake to find the two girls sitting on your outstretched arms, Beatriz on your right, Antonia on your left. You are pinned down. They are smiling mischievously into your face. You look from one to the other with a smirk. You feel certain you could shrug them off at any moment with no problem, but you like the attention and want to see what the game is, so you allow yourself to be pinned beneath them and wait.

Then Beatriz leans down and kisses you on the mouth. You feel her tongue sliding between your teeth, entering deep, exploring, and your blood leaps; you raise your face toward hers, reciprocating, but she draws away, and Antonia's face is close at the ready and her mouth dives toward yours and kisses you. You acquiesce because you can't think how else to respond, but you feel her fuzz against your lip and when her tongue snakes into your mouth, you try to jerk away, but can't because Beatriz is pushing at you from the other side. In panic, you buck and snatch your arms free and jump up.

"Cut it out!" you snap.

Antonia's wide, full-lipped mouth droops like a child's, and you try to explain it away. "I'm sorry," you say, "I just...couldn't breathe."

Beatriz's gaze, as she looks up from the blanket, is not sympathetic. "You're so *serious*," she says, and those pretty lips you have so enjoyed kissing sneer around her judgment. She sits up and hunches over her knees. Antonia blows her nose into a Kleenex.

———

The day is not much fun after that, and before long you are on the train again, headed toward the river that you will have to cross again to get home. Antonia is staying overnight with Beatriz and her cousin. When Beatriz kissed you goodbye, she held her body from you and her lips were closed and resistant, and she did not offer to walk you to the train station. You watched the two of them walk away together along Surf Avenue. Antonia had her arm around Beatriz's shoulder, whispering into her ear, making them both giggle, and you hoped Beatriz would look back, but she did not.

Now you watch out the window as the weird grinning Steeplechase face recedes, and you relive the sorrow of the moment when Beatriz said, "You're so *serious*."

The train is moving underground now, and you can no longer smell the sea, and the beautiful light of a late June day disappears as you are carried beneath the earth.

SONG OF EXPERIENCE

You emerge from the subway at 59th Street into pale, humid, westside sunlight. The year is 1973. The post-liberation, pre-AIDS decade is running its steamy course of abandon. You are 29 years old and economically free to pursue happiness. You work as a junior executive for an NGO at 10 Columbus Circle (an international association for the advancement of ethics) and earn a thousand dollars a month – more money than you ever dreamed you would be pulling in. During the 1950s you went underground and in the early '60s dropped out of college because you thought you could write your way out of sorrow, got drafted and made it out of the army before Vietnam heated up; you lived on what temp jobs netted you, ate eggs and toast or onion sandwiches on Wonder Bread three times a day, lived in cheap rooms in various cities – San Francisco, Berkeley, San Diego, Long Beach, Jackson Heights, Alphabet City, strained your eyes reading hundreds of books, dressed in Salvation Army clothing, were lonely to the point of madness, sometimes went a whole year without a woman touching you or even meeting your eyes.

In the lobby of No. 10, you step into the elevator and touch the button for your floor; the heat of your finger registers your desire to go to 9. You nod at the receptionist, an ageing Anne Landers type to whom you are an upcomling, but she knows you are he who will prevail, so doesn't make your life too difficult. You have a real job for the first time in your most of three decades. You enter your alcove, knowing that soon the woman in the office alongside will be retiring and her space will be yours. You sit at your banged up desk and think, Why not?

With money, you now have clothes, three rooms on a nice street in Jackson Heights, a brand new Chevy. You contemplate moving toTudor City, across from the U.N. Secretariat, and purchasing a Mercedes Sport SL283, preferably a candy apple convertible, white walls optional. You eat in restaurants, drink in cocktail lounges, catch Stan Getz or Tony Bennett occasionally at the Rainbow Room or Carnegie Hall, go to the theater. On the GI Bill, you are taking evening classes toward your B.A., racking up straight A's at Fordham Lincoln Center, around the corner from your Columbus Circle office, and you have four girlfriends. During the summer you have five, counting the second Susan you see once a week, Susan B., but she proves not to be content with a single day a week, so you replace her with Beth M., who is happy with whatever time you give her – this is at about the same time as Anita G. gets tired of "your games" and runs off with your prized Limited Edition copy of *The Brothers Karamazov*, a hurtful thing for her to do because she knows how much it means to you whereas she is highly unlikely ever even to crack the cover on her own. You used to read to her in bed, afterwards, recall turning her on to the scene where the bastard son makes his famous pronouncement which saved you from the death of Catholicism: *So you see, there is no god, no heaven or hell, no eternal reward or punishment, and all things are permitted.* To which Anita, a waitress from the El Inca Tavern with alluring thick lips and a million dollar smile, said, "Far out!"

You miss Anita a little bit, especially the way she liked to pretend that she didn't want to fuck and made you chase her around the apartment naked, dodging and feinting; it was fun and nice to see her from behind running away but both of you knowing that she was going to let you catch her in just a bit.

Although Beth M. is fun – she has a piquant minor masochistic streak in bed which you never realized could appeal to you – still you must admit you miss Susan B., too, and those Saturdays swimming at Jones Beach and fucking in her attic apartment in the Bronx. She lives in Parkchester, and Saturday mornings you would rise early, drive across the Bronx-Whitestone Bridge and pick her up, recross the bridge and navigate south through the arterial highways of Queens to Jacob Riis Park where the two of you would swim and frolic in the water until late afternoon. Then you would pack up and drive her home to her attic room where she smoked pot while you drank beer, listening to scratchy rock and roll records on her stereo. She had a pretty face and a big butt that turned you on, and you would start kissing, then fuck, and by midnight you were back in your Chevy, flying back across the bridge, all windows rolled down, summer night air whipping through the car, Symphony Sid blaring on the car radio. In your memory, it is always Charlie Parker blowing "Groovin' High," and you are in Jackson Heights by one to hang around in the Candlelight Inn on Nothern Boulevard and flirt with the piano bar singer there, Rosalie Z., who has the largest breasts you have ever in all your years been within arms reach of. Rosalie once told you you were a tease, all talk and no action, but you are a great believer in the old adage that a man should know his measure. By two a.m. on Saturday, the Candlelight closes, and you drive Rosalie home, kiss a little in the car (she is not really your type so you take it no further than that), then find a parking space for your Chevy and stroll home, wondering if you ought to invest in the Mercedes even though you can't really afford it. It costs five grand but you could probably sell it with little loss when you leave for Europe, which you will do before long.

Sundays you study a little, but you mostly have already read all the books during your cheap-room years in the '60s. You are majoring in Language and Literature in a special program that gives up to 40 credit points for life experience; you are counting on the full 40 because of all your years trying to learn to write and the grants you received and books you read, even though you haven't actually published anything other than letters to the editor and fillers, and you have already handed in your life experience portfolio, with full documentation (including some very flattering rejection letters from important editors like Robie Macauley and Theodore Solotaroff), to the program secretary, Barbara B., a 22-year-old former nun who is also in one of your lit classes and with whom you have a thing going on.

She leafs slowly through your life experience portfolio, which you have entitled *In Search of Understanding*.

"Think it's worth 40?" you ask.

She nods emphatically. "This is definitely a 40 portfolio," she says.

She is your height, a big girl, and normally not your type, but she unexpectedly rang the bell of your apartment one day, asked if she could come in, and started crying because, she said, she had just come from a ménage à trois that she had not wanted to be involved in and she needed a friend to talk to. She said that she came to you because she trusted you ever since Professor James, a spiffy modern poetry prof who wears two-tone shoes, had asked you – because you sometimes spoke up in class – to come up front and read "The Love Song of J. Alfred Prufrock" aloud, apparently thinking this would intimidate you, although he could not have known that you knew "Prufrock" practically by heart. Barbara said she was moved by the sensitive, confident way you'd read it, which had given her the confidence to come to you when she needed help. So the two of you started talking and then you started kissing, and that is how that thing started, and now Barbara comes over most Sunday afternoons, and the two of you cook and hear music and drink cheap New York State champagne and fuck.

(To your surprise you learn that the ménage à trois was with two other women, one of whom is a nun and the other your philosophy professor, who does not at all look like someone who would have a ménage a trois; she's about fifty and looks rather matronly, although you begin to look more closely at the shape beneath her matronly dresses and win new respect for it and begin to regret that you declined a few months before when you were in her office after class and she offered you a cognac (Carte Noir!) Maybe she wanted to have a ménage à trois with you, and that is definitely one of the yet-unfulfilled items on your Life List. However, you do not know what you think about one of the threesome having been an active nun. Barbara's nun career was brief – she left before taking her vow of chastity – but all you can think of with regard to active nuns is none of this and none of that, and of Sister Mary Alequo's glittering eyes in 1955 as she told your 5th grade class that 99.9 percent of people in mental institutions were there because of violations of the sixth and ninth commandments. But what the hell? All things are permitted now, regardless of race, religion, creed or sexual preference.)

You liked having that Susan-Barbara structure to your weekends. It made you feel secure. But one Saturday when you drove Susan B. back to her attic apartment in Parkchester, she seemed particularly uncommunicative. Truly she never talked much anyway, which was quite okay with you; you've never had any trouble filling the silence, but this day she was particularly laconic if not downright sullen, so finally you had to ask her if something was wrong. She didn't answer. You asked if she was unhappy about something. She didn't respond. You reached to her to offer physical comfort, but she jerked away and moved up flush against the passenger door with her face turned away from you. You drove on in silence and parked outside her house in the summer dusk. You considered asking if it was that time of month, except in your experience that question, especially if it *is* that time of month, was likely to earn you a song from the warm lands. So you tried being more concrete. You asked, "Aren't you happy with this arrangement?"

Now she looked at you, but her expression was not all that friendly. "Ar*range*ment!" she sneered and got out of the car, smacking the door shut. She walked to the side entrance which led to the attic staircase without looking back at you, and you heard the door slam shut after her. You put the car in gear and pulled away.

That night on the Bronx Whitestone Bridge, Symphony Sid played Coltrane blowing "The Damned Don't Cry," followed by "Here's That Rainy Day," and Rosalie had called in sick to the Candlelight Inn, and everything generally felt like shit, but you stopped off at Budd's on 37th Avenue for a nightcap, and a girl sitting alone at the bar started to catapult peanuts at you with her swizzle stick, and the two of you got to chatting. Her name was Beth, and you invited her home at closing time. There, she allowed you the privilege of being the first boy (she calls men "boys") ever to go down on her. Although at 24 she was not a virgin, she was afraid for some reason to be gone down on, so you had to calm and reassure her first which became a rather piquant challenge, and then suddenly she screamed like a jungle parrot and shouted, "Oh god, I came! I finally came!"

Early the following Saturday morning, you picked her up and drove her out to Oyster Bay where you swam in the Long Island sound and ate clams before coming back to your place, and she became your regular Saturday date.

Next afternoon, Barbara came over, and you broiled two thick steaks and tossed a salad with balsamico vinegar and virgin olive oil and heated a baguette and you drank two bottles of wine between you, and she took superior position in the sack, which you had to admit she was quite proficient at.

During the week, you have an hour between the end of your workday and your first evening class at Fordham during which you generally go to O'Neal's Baloon across from Lincoln Center where you sit at the bar and drink a double Dewar's or two and watch water bubble in the Lincoln Center fountain and the opera house with its Chagall murals. O'Neal's Baloon used to be called O'Neal's Saloon until somebody discovered an old city ordinance that prohibited any saloon within a four-block radius of a church, and St. Luke's is three blocks away from O'Neal's, so Mr. O'Neal had to change the name of the place which he did by converting the 'S' in "Saloon" to a 'B'. And that is why the Baloon in O'Neal's Baloon is spelled with a single 'l'. That's a little-known piece of '70s Manhattan history for you.

Classes are normally two hours, from six to eight, and sometimes, afterwards, you go up to Germantown for a beer at the Finn Inn. You once met a woman there who became interested when you said you were studying at Fordham; she revealed to you her ambition of being the first woman to become a Catholic priest, and the two of you ended at closing time sitting on the front stoop of a brownstone making out. Until she found out you were at Fordham Lincoln Center and not Rose Hill, which she judged meant you had no pull with the Jesuits after all, and she left you sitting on the brownstone stoop in a highly aroused state beneath a four a.m. drizzle.

More often, though, you visit Susan MacG. on W. 102nd or May Anne M. on E. 88th.

May Anne is difficult. She is a 26-year-old virgin and a close friend of Barbara B. Barbara tells you, in sworn confidence, that May Anne was also a nun, for several years. You believe it. You don't much like visiting May Anne because she has a Siamese cat who hates you and once leaped on your head and started scratching for blood. Fortunately you got your hands up in time and they took the brunt of the scratches. You were in bed at the time with May Anne who wants to lose her virginity but wants to do so stepwise, by gentle degrees. At that time she was at the naked-to-panties-and-petting phase, but you had to promise not to try to remove the panties or to touch her in the panties zone. In fact, you were not particularly inclined to try to remove her panties or to touch her in their zone (you did not even know quite why you were there other than that you always had a weakness for half-naked women who wanted sex, even if stepwise by gentle degree) and lost even more interest after that Siamese Satan leapt on your head. May Anne put on her very unsexy bathrobe and bandaged your hands in the bathroom, and you had to get a tetanus shot next day.

You do not have great hopes for the future of your relationship with May Anne, which is too bad, because in a way you like her more than any of the others. She is a poet, a pretty good one, and a good conversationalist with an interesting mind and, as mentioned, has expressed the wish eventually to have sex with you. But she is a complicated woman.

Less complicated, although not without complications, is your relationship with the other Susan – Susan MacG., recently of Glasgow. She has a Glaswegian accent which is a very large turn-on, and she's long and lean and definitely has a European attitude toward sex – i.e., that it is good to fuck. The only drawback with Susan MacG. is that she also has a pet, an Airedale, and she only has one room and doesn't want to lock the "poor thing" in the bathroom when you fuck. Unlike, the Siamese Satan, this Airedale is fond of you and gets excited when you go at it with his mistress and wants to get into the act with his kinky-furry head. Susan MacG. can hold him off the bed with a sharp command, but she cannot stop him excitedly nibbling at your toes at inopportune moments.

Nothing is simple, as old O. Jones used to say when he tried to waltz, drunk, on the slippery stones.

But come June, you will have earned enough credits – counting the 40 for your life experience portfolio, which Barbara

B. has convinced you will be yours – for your B.A., and your boss, a childless maternal spinster of sixty who seems to regard you as the son she never had, has offered you a posting to France then – dependent, though, upon your having earned the B.A.

So all you have to do is find interesting ways to pass the time between now and then. It's good you didn't invest in the Mercedes, after all, or moved to Tudor City. You already have a buyer for your Chevy, have given notice to your landlord and have sorted through your meager possessions, have someone interested in the odd sticks of furniture you have accumulated. Essentially, all you will have to do, when the time comes to take off, is pack your clothes and books in the steamer trunk you bought for a sawbuck from the superintendent's basement stock of left-behind articles.

It comforts you to think that you will be living in Europe away from all the complications of your life. Beth is unhappy about your plans to leave, which only goes to show that you should never tell anyone anything. She is the only one you mentioned it to, and right away, instead of being happy for you, she began to cry. You hate it when women cry. Sometimes you even feel they do it out of spite because they sense that you are emotionally stunted and have not cried since you were a child. What can you do when a woman cries? Stroke her and say, There there? Promise to do whatever it is that she might wish you to do – although in this case it would mean not moving to France, and there is no way you intend not to do that and further no way that you intend to spend the rest of your life with Beth. Beth is cute and nice and funny and intelligent, a great reader, albeit a college drop-out, with a sexy body, and she always laughs at your jokes in a sincere manner, which is important. And, as mentioned, she has this minor masochistic streak and suggests certain things that are rather exciting to both of you. That alone is a particularly strong quality in a woman. Also, she likes to drink just as much as you. So Beth is a woman to be thankful for, and you are thankful, but not to the extent that you will change your long-term plans and give up your European posting.

You spend more and more time with her as autumn moves on and through the winter and spring. You both like jazz and go to the Outside Inn on Saturday evenings to hear the trio there, and from time to time, her palm resting on your thigh, she whispers something she wants you to do to her later and gets you so steamy your eyeglasses fog, and soon Anita P. and Susan M. are but vague memories, and you're less interested in seeing May Anne or Susan MacG., although Susan does have a couple of moves you miss, but then again, you think of the Airedale, and the two things cancel each other out, and it is much simpler to see Beth, so you begin to come back to Jackson Heights most nights after class and meet Beth, whose moves are every bit as good as Susan MacG.'s and who dreams up games to play and household implements to employ that teach you new respect for her imagination and nerve, your own being paltry by comparison.

Then Beth finds out about Barbara B. You never kept Barbara a secret, but neither did you ever tell Beth about her. The way she finds out is that she comes over one Monday evening and discovers a brassiere in the bathroom – why Barbara left her brassiere in the bathroom you do not know, nor do you know what she wore home, although bras had been burned and abandoned in the previous decade and are by no means requisite any longer. In any event, Beth begins to cry which is worse than if she got mad. At least if she got mad, you could get mad back, but what can you do about crying? Cry back?

Comforted by the fact that you never used the 'L' word (in truth, you were tempted once or twice to say it to May Anne, of all people, when the two of you were deep in conversation, but you refrained) you try to explain to Beth that neither of you ever said anything about exclusivity and that anyway you will be moving to Europe soon, and the last thing in the world you would ever wish to do is to hurt her, but then she is just crying harder, and finally she goes into the bathroom, comes out again, still crying, pulls on her dungaree jacket and lets herself out. You watch her walk down the hallway to the elevator, still sniffling and blowing her nose, and you call her back, but she doesn't look at you or answer, and when the elevator door closes after her, you go back into your apartment and sit in your butterfly chair with your face in your palms and wish to hell you could cry like that, maybe it would be a release, maybe it would put an end to this horrible feeling of shittiness that has overcome you so that everything seems just all fucked up.

Next day in class, Barbara asks if you will have a drink with her afterwards, and the two of you go over to O'Neal's Baloon, where she tells you that May Anne is upset that you've stopped calling her. She says that May Anne doesn't know you are also seeing *her*, even though *she* doesn't mind that you're seeing *May Anne*. In fact, she wouldn't want to come between the two of you; and if she is the reason you've stopped calling May Anne, she is prepared to step aside.

You're thinking that if everybody takes that attitude, you're going to end up all alone, a situation you experienced back in the '60s and did not like one little bit.

"The thing is," Barbara says, "that you are all May Anne has. She even told me that in those very words: He is all I have."

"Well," you say, picking a lingering scrap of scab from the back of your hand, "she has the cat, too."

"But that's not the same," says Barbara. "Do you still have feelings for her?"

You shrug ruefully which you hope will convey a satisfactory message since you do not know what to say. You're wondering to what extent you *ever* had *actual* feelings for her, although there were those moments in conversation where you glimpsed the deeps of her mind. But still. For a moment, you almost say to Barbara, "I have more feelings for you," but that might lead to even worse misunderstandings, and you are wondering if it is you yourself who has misunderstood things. Maybe you have misunderstood everything, and you are thinking more and more how good it is that within a few weeks you will be on your way to France.

Then Barbara drops the bomb. "There's something else."

You order another double Dewars on the rocks and a white wine for Barbara, and she mercifully does not continue until the drinks are served.

"Your life experience portfolio came back from Jim P. – the evaluator? He told me he was planning to give it a 32 and asked what I thought. I told him I thought you deserved way more than that, and he listened, but he only raised it to a 38."

Which means that you will be two credits short of your B.A. in June. No. B.A. means no posting in France. And you already gave notice on your apartment (and it has already been rented to a new tenant as of July 1st), already sold your car, at a loss, to an Iranian exchange student, and your life in general is not otherwise particularly tidy either.

Barbara touches the back of your hand. She looks a bit like a larger, slightly porcine version of Shirley Maclaine, that kind of dark short hair, pretty mouth, upturned nose. You squeeze her hand, thinking, Your place or mine?

"But there's a happy ending," she says then and smiles. "He wrote the 38 on the front page in pencil and gave the portfolio to me for final processing. So I erased the 38 and wrote in a 40. *Basta!*"

"Won't he find out?"

She shakes her head. "He's already forgotten the whole matter. The only thing he thinks about is hitting on me and every other secretary in the college."

"You would do that for me?" you ask, your eyes filling.

She meets your gaze and says, "I love you." She says it not portentously, like a declaration of love, but matter-of-factly, more like something obvious and well-known. You don't know if your face sags as much as it feels like it does, but you see a flicker of emotion mirrored in her grey eyes, just a flicker, and then she says, "Don't worry. I don't expect anything."

That Sunday afternoon, she doesn't appear at your apartment as she usually does, and next evening, you learn that she quit her job without notice and moved back to Michigan. You ask for her forwarding address but are told by the other administrator that that is confidential information. The other administrator is a nun with a wisp of tan hair showing beneath the kerchief she wears on her head, and her eyes are small and dark as they stare at you. You wonder whether this is the nun who was the third person in the ménage á trois. You shudder.

You receive your degree in June, *summa cum laude*, and you skip the graduation ceremony in order to pack your steamer trunk and have it collected by the shipping company. The phone will not be disconnected until the end of the day. You could still say your goodbyes – if there were anyone to say goodbye to.

THAT NIGHT ON THE FARM

The season is spring, the setting Celtic, the year 1978, the day a rare Dublin Saturday with sunlight glinting on the Liffey as it flows beneath the O'Connell Street Bridge. A tinker girl holding a baby with soot-smudged face in her shawl sits against the abutment, shaking a paper cup. You drop a five p. coin into the cup and decide to change direction. You were headed north over the bridge, but instead follow your feet south across the river in search of what the day might offer.

You have a room at Trinity, in Building 38, the very room in which J. P. Donleavy stayed when he studied there under the G.I. Bill in the '40s, and you have the remainder of Saturday and Sunday morning free, your conference having ended the night before. The flight back to Copenhagen was cheaper if you stayed the weekend, even with the extra expense of lodging and meals.

You have an idea for the perfect gift for your wife and turn toward Nassau Street, past the sculpture of Molly Malone with her wheelbarrow ("The Tart with the Cart"), follow along the grey stone wall of Trinity to Merrion Square, turn left, then left again to No. 1 Lincoln Place, and are cheered to see that Sweny's Chemist is still open. You let yourself into the little shop and browse among the wares on display, finding just what you hoped you might: a fist-sized lump of Bronnley's lemon soap, wrapped in tissue. You lift it to your nose and sniff the lemony aroma, imagining your way back to June 16th, 1904, the fictional day when Leopold Bloom bought just the same soap from just this same shop for his wife, Molly, even as he knew she was preparing to commit adultery with Blazes Boylon.

"Is it for herself?" asks the twinkly-eyed old woman from behind the ancient wooden desk, and you smile, nod, pay, and store the lump of tissue-wrapped soap in your hip pocket in honor of Poldy, poor peaceful contemplative cuckold Jew.

On the street, you pause, staring across at Kennedy's Public House and wonder what your wife will make of your giving her a bar of soap famous for having been given to the adulteress Molly. But the soap was a symbol of Leopold's great love for Molly, despite all. No need to go into the details; she'll love it.

Now it is nearing noon, soon lunchtime, but your belly is still content from breakfast at Trinity's Buttery: eggs, rashers and sausage, black and white pudding, fried mushroom and tomato, baked beans and toast. All that was lacking was a pint, which you will soon remedy.

Your shoes walk you riverward again, along Duke, past The Duke and The Bailey and Davy Byrnes, left on Grafton past Bewley's, right on Harry Street past McDaid's, and left past the Brazen Arms. All fine public houses, but there's another you have thought of that you'd like to visit, through Dame Court, across Dame Street, down Temple Lane, you enter the Temple Bar in Temple Bar, where you can sit out in the open sunny courtyard with your pint of the black stuff and, with luck, might wrangle a glass of potjeen from the barman.

You take a high stool alongside a barrel and contemplate the antique tin signs mounted on the walls, advertising Poser's Whiskey, Bagot's Hutton & Co. Fine Old Whiskey/Murphy's/From the Wood that's Good, Bulmer's: Nothing Added but Time,

Crested Ten: John Jameson & Son, Murphy's Extra Stout: On Draught and In Bottle, Lady's Well Brewery-Cork, Cantwell's Café au lait... *Whiskey, it keepeth the rason from stifling.*

You quaff your black stuff and, sighing, wipe your mouth with the back of your hand, ready for another, and as you rise you notice a young woman seated just around the corner of a wooden pillar, dark-haired and blue-eyed, lovely combination, wearing tight faded jeans and a tee shirt of ponderous contours. She is reading *The New Yorker* and nursing the skimpy remains of a pint of lager.

"*New Yorker!*" you exclaim. "Makes me homesick."

"For New York?"

"Born and raised there." You neglect to specify in Queens. "Yourself?"

"Cleveland."

"Largest Slovenian population in the world outside of Slovenia."

She sits up in her chair, affording a fine view of her allurements, blushing with what appears to be pleasure. "Lived there all my life, and I didn't know that!"

"Just shtick with me, kid," you say. "You'll learn lots you didn't know."

She laughs merrily, and you can see how young she is, and you wonder what in the world you are doing, but choose not to pursue that particular question just now, not just yet. Instead, you say, "Another pint?"

She looks at her glass as though she hadn't noticed it was empty; then: "Sure. Okay. Thanks."

Inside, the barman, with a twisted nose and a sweet smile, looks at you and barks, "Talk to me!"

You order a pint of harp and another of the black stuff, spot a sign offering half a dozen river oysters for a pittance and order them, too. You pay, but keep your wallet out. "You know what – I'd also like two small potjeens."

"If it's potjeen you're after you'll have to go to the Garda. They've confiscated it all."

You lean close across the bar, speak softly, "My girl and I have to go back later today, and we haven't even tasted it and would so very much like to. Could you help us?"

"The two of you come over together, did you?" he says with a smirk.

You smile, shrug.

He steps away from the bar and returns with a tumblerful of clear spirit which he sets before you.

"How much do I owe you?" you ask.

"Can't sell it to you. Illegal."

You put a handful of coins on the bar, and he says, "That's grand. I'll bring your oysters out to you."

"Won't we have a lovely time," you say to the girl, balancing the three glasses over the threshold to the courtyard, "drinking whiskey gin and wine, on Coronation day."

The barman comes out afterwards and lays a plate of half shells on the barrel head, along with brown bread and butter. "Get it down your necks now," he says, "it's good for you."

The young woman looks skeptically at the oysters. You squeeze on lemon, scoop one off the shell on the blade of the knife, cutting the muscle free beneath the hinge, and mouthe it down, drink the juice from the shell and wash it back with potjeen. Then you scoop another onto the blade and hold it out to her, cupping your free hand beneath it. Her eyes meet yours. She looks at the cup of your left, turns your hand in hers and looks at the ring. "What?" she asks. "You're married?"

"Yes," you say and meet her gaze, still holding the oyster on the blade. She studies you for a moment, a smile pursing her lips. Then she opens her mouth and delivers it to you for the oyster. She closes her eyes, smiling, hums with pleasure, and you hold the glass of potjeen to her.

"Enhances the taste," you say and lean forward to kiss her.

She is twenty-one years old, thirteen years your junior. She is in her last year at the American College of Dublin on Merrion Square. She dances ballet. Neither of you again mentions the fact that you are married. You take her back to Trinity with you, through the brick portal where a sign says, "Cyclists Dismount," and across the cobblestoned square to Building 38 and into your high-ceilinged, tall-windowed room where you undress and admire one another and partake of each other's bodies. Then you share the sharp cheddar and stilton and biscuits and burgundy remaining in your larder, and she produces a joint which you smoke before another, slower partaking of one another. You marvel at the block-like structure of her feet, misshapen from years of dancing ballet.

A little before ten, she says she has to leave if she is to make curfew, kisses your mouth, takes one final smiling look into your eyes and is gone. No names, no addresses, no phone numbers.

The room has grown dark through the afternoon and evening. She left a roach in the ashtray. Using your tie clasp as a roach clip, you get three small hits out of it and lie on the bed with your fingers over your mouth. They smell of lemon and oyster and cunt, and as your exhileration begins to fade, you try to remember a question that had popped into your head earlier, but has been eluding you all day.

The flight to Copenhagen next day is on Aer Lingus. You sit in the back rows, where you can smoke, and you drink vodka for the two hours it takes back to Kastrup, turning the Bronnley's lemon soap over and over in your hands, its fresh, innocent scent lifting to your nose.

You are home by five p.m.. Your wife greets you with a kiss, sniffs, says, "Vodka."

"I had one on the plane."

She has made fresh liver paste and baked rye bread for dinner – things she knows you love. She is delighted with the lemon soap, which you tell her Leopold bought for Molly in 1904. You do not tell the details of what Molly did that day while Leopold wandered through Dublin. You tell the story of your own week in that city, the Joyce conference, and of the nice long walk you took on your free day. You tell it just as it happened, though you eliminate one character from the cast.

You also bought a full bottle of Carte Noir from duty free, and your wife makes coffee and has a little bakery box of petit fours which you take on the balcony to your apartment which looks down the hilly street to the castle gardens. The sky is still light at this time of year. You can see the green copper towers of the castle, and you toast with your snifters and smoke cigarettes and she smells her hands, which she has washed with Bronnley's lemon soap, and hums with pleasure at the smell, and then the two of you fall silent.

You are thinking dangerous thoughts that you do not wish to think. You think about the four years of your marriage, the three apartments the two of you have lived in, each one a little better than the last. You think about the wild years you lived before you left new York and how you had believed you'd left all that behind. You think about how easily this thing happened yesterday, how you made it happen, no one to blame but yourself, and you did it without a thought. First chance you really had in four years, and you grabbed it without a thought, went directly to action. Is that what your marriage vows are worth? you wonder.

You caution yourself not to be rash, not to tell her, but you fear the whole story tells itself on your lying, adulterous face.

Your wife sits in shadow on the balcony, barely visible in the flickering of the dish of votive candles she has lit on the table between you. It occurs to you how quiet she has been since you got home, how quiet and loving. Which is not really like her. She is not the tender-hearted sort, is a professional woman, has to make it in a man's world.

She reaches for the Carte Noir. "May I?" she asks, holding it over her empty snifter.

That's not like her either. You nod. "Of course."

She tops you up, then pours for herself, re-corks the bottle and says, "Henrik stopped by."

"Henrik?"

"You remember, our neighbor from the north side? The guy who was married to the Polish woman?"

"Oh, Henrik. Haven't seen him in years. How is he? What'd he want?"

"I had to ask him to leave."

"Really? Why?"

She inhales deeply. "There's something I have to tell you. I hope you will listen all the way before you react."

You stare at her. Then she is telling you about something that happened more than three years ago, not a year after you married. She reminds you of the time you and she went to a summer party at a farm on Funen. The dinner was held in a renovated barn. There were many guests. The girl seated beside you was flirting, and you danced a couple of times with her, and your wife was tipsy and got furious and stormed out into the fields, and you couldn't find her. You sat alone on a bench and felt miserable. Nothing had happened with the girl – you only danced with her, but you were sad that you'd made your wife, your new bride, jealous and unhappy. So you sat on the bench, waiting for her to return, and drank bottles of beer in the steeping dusk while people danced in the barn and ran around the farmyard, lauging and kissing and drinking green bottles of beer, and rock blasted from the big speakers that had been set up.

Finally your wife showed up and apologized for getting so jealous, and you went up to the room you'd been given – a room you shared, you remember now, with Henrik and his Polish wife. The Polish wife had gone to bed early, and now Henrik was there with her, too, and they were making love, and you and your wife crawled into a sleeping bag and made love, too. It was kind of piquant, making love in the same room with the other couple.

"Where were you all that time you were gone?" you ask now. "I never figured that out. You were gone for two or three hours."

"I was with Henrik," she says. "I was drunk." She lowers her eyes. "He fucked me." She looks at your face again. "I'm laying my cards on the table and hoping you will forgive me."

"What did he want when he came by now?"

"He's called me a couple of times since that night, wanted to see me. I told him it was out of the question. He called again on Saturday and wanted to come over, but I told him you were away, and it was out of the question. He suggested that you could sleep with his wife."

"Is that what you want?"

"Of course not! I hung up on him, I was so pissed off, and he just came over. I didn't let him in. I told him to go away. I'm hoping that telling you about this, that you can forgive me."

You reach for the Carte Noir and refill your glass, reach to pour for her, light a cigarette.

"Will you forgive me?" she asks. "I took the chance of telling you. I hoped we could wipe the slate clean."

"Just let me absorb this first, okay?"

"When a person asks for forgiveness," she says, "it's *cheap* not to give it." You can hear that she's getting mad now, which she has no grounds to. You have no grounds to be righteous either, but this has all flooded in on you, and you have to absorb it. You cannot help but think of the fact that when you and she made love that night on the farm that Henrik's cock had been there first. You wonder if he came in her, if she at least washed herself. You think about the fact that Henrik and *his* wife were making love in the same room as the two of you and what was he thinking about as he fucked his wife and you fucked yours, that he had been there first that night, and you were getting sloppy seconds?

What right do you have?

You shield your eyes with your palm and say, "It's okay. I forgive you. I just need time to absorb this."

"Come to bed," she says. "Make love to me."

"Please, I need a little time. You go in. I'll be in in a while. Let me smoke a cigarette and absorb this."

"Don't be like that," she says and stubs out her own cigarette. "Let's put this behind us. Forgive and forget. Don't be cheap."

"I can't make love to you right at this minute. I need a little time. Please, just go in. I'll be in later."

"Fuck you," she says, and her feet are hard across the floor. The bedroom door slams after her.

You stand by the railing of the little balcony and smoke another cigarette, looking out at the dim gloomy evening like a dusky land of dreams. You flip your cigarette into the darkness and go in to the bathroom. The lemon soap is still wet in the soap dish on the sink. You can smell it. You brush your teeth, wash your hands and face with the soap, stand in the hall looking at the bedroom door, decide to have another cognac and a cigarette. From your chair on the balcony, you can see the bedroom door. You wonder if you have waited too long, ruined something. You think about Henrik, whose face you cannot quite recall, a tallish skinny guy, try to picture him fucking her in the fields. Now you're getting mad, but remember then what you were doing yesterday. It seems strange that the pleasures of that Saturday have now lost their luster. Maybe it's not too late to go in to her, but you don't rise. Not yet. You just want to run it through your mind one more time, try to think it all through clearly.

IN TURKU IT IS SNOWING

———

Beneath the Cretan sun perhaps you have a chance, the four of you. At just this moment, it seems so, in the pool of the Blue Triton Hotel in Agios Nikolaos as your wife lounges with a book in the shade of a large white umbrella and you play with your two angels in the water: Nikolai, seven, and Simone, five. With them is a shy, chubby boy of nine, who has gravitated toward you. He is a Dane, like your wife and kids, here alone with his mother who like most people these days is separated from her husband. You were also separated from Liv for a few weeks this spring; then your mother died, and Liv let you come home.

Now you float on your back in the pool, paddling your arms, your right toe thrust up like a weapon that the three kids gigglingly flee from. This game was born of your wife's complaint over the breakfast buffet this morning that last night in bed you'd scratched her leg with your toe nails.

"They're razor sharp!" she said with disgust.

Embarrassed, you turned it into a game, singing to the tune of the Zorro TV theme song:

> *Out of the night*
> *comes Toe-o!*
> *Razor sharp,*
> *Oh no-o!*

Despairing of evading your newly clipped toe, the kids climb to the poolside patio and challenge you to wrestle. You breech and offer to take all three of them on at once with one hand behind your back. They love this advantage – inch toward you, eager mischief plastered on their smiles, little pink claws clutching tentatively, threateningly toward you. Three Greek men swim to the side of the pool and hang from the edge, chins propped on hands to observe the combat – this is serious business, an old guy challenged by three kids. You had planned to let the kids win, but public honor is involved now as the four of you grapple on the slippery tiles. Finally, with a cry of defeat, you topple but scoop them along with you into the chlorine drink.

Surfacing, you glance at Liv to see if she is glad as you are at this moment. But even here in the sunny south islands, her smile has that same northern winter distance. She has been unhappy for so long, perhaps always, even back when so much seemed so possible. Perhaps you only fooled yourself that she could be happy with you in a way she had not been with her parents or with the lawyer who broke their engagement and her heart.

Your life together began to sour five years ago, sometime after your little girl was born. Why? When? Perhaps when you each began to see that the other would never change. That Liv's smile would always be distant and troubled, that she would always have a stormy temper and that you would always be – what? – whatever it is that you are. In truth perhaps it was wrong from the start. But if you had never started, then Nikolai and Simone would not exist. Your world as such is unimaginable without Nikolai and Simone.

A few days after you moved out on Liv, you knew that you had made a mistake that you needed to try to undo. You knew this the evening that you phoned home to say goodnight to your kids and your mother-in-law answered. You like your mother-in-law, but when you said you'd like to speak to your son, she said, "I don't know." And in that simple phrase, you instantly understood that there would now be barriers between you and your kids, barriers that did not exist before and that should never exist. With a cold, quiet force that knew no doubt, you said, "Put my son on the phone," and she did so without further resistance.

"I miss you, son," you said.

"I miss you, too, Dad. I lay in bed at night, and I think, *Dad! Dad! Dad!...*" At that moment you knew that the problems you and your wife had been experiencing for several years and the feelings that had developed between you and another woman over the past year were without meaning compared to the need to remove the barriers that were arising between you and your children.

When you were their age, life without your father or mother was unimaginable, especially your mother, but your father died years ago, and your mother died last April. What a month to die. So many seas away she died. The phone rang at two in the morning – Liv had given your cell number; you were awakened in the bed of your new woman – and you listened to your brother explain that earlier that evening your mother had told him, "I have the worst headache I ever had." She lay down on the sofa and began to writhe and then was still. A stroke. In the hospital, they put her on a resuscitator. That's where it was now, they were taking EEGs to measure her brain response. You told him you would take the first plane, and within ten hours, you were hanging in an iron corridor over the Atlantic, just a few hours from your dying mother, remembering twenty years before when your father died, also suddenly, though not unexpectedly -- he had used himself too hard. What you did not know was that as you sat on the plane, your brother was giving the okay to turn off the resuscitator. By the time you got to New York, the undertaker was already embalming her.

"Her brain was dead," your brother said. " But don't worry, just in case, I whispered in her ear that you were on the way."

At the funeral, you sat in the pew gazing at the flower-draped coffin which contained the body of your mother and remembered how as a boy you used to fear her death. When you were Nikolai's age. You hadn't feared divorce – that was beyond imagining. Yet now you had abandoned them both.

Afterwards there was a get together at a local bar and grill, and your brother called you aside to hand you a copy of the new will. "Mother wanted me to have the house," he explained. "And everything in it. After all, I was the one who stayed with her."

Instead of asking him if that wasn't making a virtue of a weakness, you said, "Well I would really like to have one of those antique cut-glass crystal bowls she was so fond of. And a few of the books and maybe…"

"Everything in the apartment," he repeated, "means *everything*. That's how Mother wanted it. But you will always be welcome to come over and look at the things. This is for you," he added and held out a sealed business envelope. You didn't open it until you were on the plane. There was a check in it, his personal check. For ten thousand dollars. On a yellow post-it was written, "Mother wanted us all to share the remaining cash." For a moment you considered hiring a lawyer, contesting it, but what you did was order a double vodka on the rocks from the stewardess to numb your sudden understanding of the futility of fighting the past.

Your flight back to Denmark was diverted because of a ground crew strike, and you had to overnight in transit in Finland. In Turku. It was snowing. You sat in the window of your hotel room and watched flake after flake melt in the Abu River's icy mouth, remembering your mother's face in the casket. The undertaker had apologized that the resuscitator had distorted her mouth so it seemed to be frowning; he had employed all his art but had been unable to wipe the frown away. With a lip liner pencil, your sister tried to draw a gentler expression on your mother's dead lips, and watching her do so, you began to snigger but ended hugging her, the two of you crying, while your brother stood to the side. "I have some things to take care of," he said.

Your mother never knew that you and Liv had separated, but the frown made you wonder. In the room in Turku, you phoned the woman you had loved for the past year, whom you had moved in with three weeks ago. You told her that you loved her, that you loved her more than you had ever loved another woman, but that you were going back to your wife, that you had to.

"You should do it then," she said quietly.

You were unaware of whether the depth of love you felt for her was true. Hadn't you felt that same love for Liv at the start? You could not remember. Perhaps if you had met this woman first... But such speculation was pointless because if you had met another woman, then Nikolai and Simone would not exist now, and your world is no longer imaginable without Nikolai and Simone.

"I shouldn't take you back," Liv said. "I really should not take you back. What you have done is unforgiveable."

"I made a mistake," you said.

You made so many mistakes, but could you really have done anything differently? The only thing you were certain of at that moment was that you desperately, at whatever cost, wanted to be with your children, to share their childhood with them, to be a father for them, living in the same house with them.

The chubby nine-year-old's name is Lars, and you and Liv invite him and his mother to have dinner with you on the waterfront. The sun is still shining, and the six of you sit beneath the open-walled straw roof of a Taverna, enjoying the breeze off the harbor, eating Greek salads and Tsatziki, grilled swordfish steaks, sipping chilled retsina. For dessert there are fancy ice cream concoctions with tiny paper umbrellas stuck in them; the kids collect the umbrellas from the adults' desserts. How delighted they are to have all those tiny paper umbrellas on toothpicks; they sit opening and closing them, holding them over their heads and giggling. Then, with a supply of coins, they abandon the paper umbrellas for the electronic games while the three adults sit and chat over strong coffee and Metaxa.

Most of the chatting is done in Danish by Liv and Lars's mother. Your Danish is good enough, but at the moment you prefer to gaze out over the harbor and think. The dark has come down suddenly, as it does in the south, and there is half a moon riding in crackled bits on the undulating surface of the water. You think about the fact that your children prefer you to speak Danish with them, despite your heavy accent, even when you read to them at bedtime, even *Alice in Wonderland – Alice I Eventyrland*, which is a terrible translation. You consider the chance turnings that led you across the sea to another country, to have children for whom you speak a broken language. You smile, remembering the test you gave your son a while ago to see if he had picked up any English. You said to him, in English, "Nikolai, go in and tell your mother that the coffee is ready." Nikolai went in and what you heard him say was: "Mutta! Kaffe ess rrread-ee!"

You order another round of Metaxa – this time with several more stars – and gazing contentedly around you in the summer dark you take in details. An olive tree, a blossoming rhododendron, other flowers and plants you cannot name. Liv would be able to – she would know the oregano, the rosemary, the chamomile, the lavender, thyme, fennel… She would break off leaves of this and that, crumble them between her fingers so that you could smell the various spicy aromas. It occurs to you that you know more about brandy than you do about plants and flowers, and you realize this says something about you and about the difference between you and Liv. You would be hard pressed to tell a Cedar from a Cypress, but you know your Cognac from your Armagnac, your Courvoisier from your Carte Noir. You are, after all, your father's son. For that matter, like him, you can quote dozens of poems by heart, but to begin to do so is the quickest way to evoke Liv's ire.

How different the two of you are.

How different your mother and father were. How different Liv's mother and father are.

You recall one evening in New York when you were back for your mother's funeral, your sister told you that your father had confided in her shortly before he died that your mother and he had not made love – had "sexual relations" she said – in twenty years. Apparently she had not thought this out before telling you, but you had always been quick at arithmetic; you had been twenty years old when your father died. Figure it out. Do the math. So what came first, Dad's alcoholism or the cessation of Mom's desire? You recall – how could you forget? – the day you came home from school. – you were eight – to find your father stumbling around the house, hallucinating. You learned later what he was seeing: writhing insects in his coffee, snarling red-eyed dogs in the hall, a long dead aunt in the doorway, and he saw Jesus. Your sister told you the doctor had said that was a sign of an extremely good person – to have religious delusions under the DTs.

You do not wish to think about this now, but cannot help thinking about the fact that you and Liv have not have sex in at least five years. You focus instead on the lovely Cretan evening, you want to experience your kids' delight. The three of you stroll back to the hotel beneath the glittering black canopy of sky, straggling behind the three children who are by turns awed by and irreverent of their surroundings, hopping boisterously onto a fence, kneeling reverently to peer into a green hedge to inspect a bird's nest. Liv and Lars's mother still chat, how endless the well of their chatter seems. The sound of it is comforting as the sound of the children's shrieks and whispers, the occasional waiter who bids you, "Good evenink!" before trying to tempt you in for a late supper or nightcap. The nightcap tempts you, but you remember the balcony of your hotel apartment, planning a nightcap for Liv and yourself after the children have been placed between crisp white sheets and sung and read to.

The dark breeze is constant, feathery, and you send a silent prayer to your mother for the ten thousand she left you. Never mind all the rest. All the *things*. Your brother is welcome to them, a 50-year-old bachelor, an orphan really, parentless and childless, mateless. The ten thousand is already spent – on an electric lawn mower, a new garden table and chairs, and this vacation. Thank you, Mom. It was just what we needed.

The kids sunburned faces asleep against the white sheets, they don't even snore, their sleeping breath a whisper, and you carry two ouzos out to the balcony and stand beneath the sky. You think of Odysséas Elytis, of Nikos Kazantzakis, both born here, of Theodorákis born of Cretan parents, persecuted by the Colonels for his politics, his music banned. You think of Georgios Seféris, also born here, who won the Nobel Prize in 1963.

Hearing Liv behind you, you turn and begin, "And if the soul is ever to know itself/It must gaze into the soul…"

Her dark eyes glare at you, and her lips are pressed so tight together that they are circled white. *"Don't!"* she hisses.

"That was Seféris. He won…"

"Do *not* try to teach me!" she snaps.

"Right," you mutter, startled, seeking sarcasm as a shield. "What could be worse than us teaching each other something?"

"Your behavior tonight was inexcusable!"

"What?"

"You heard me. You didn't say a word all night. I bet you don't even know Lars's mother's name, do you? Do you? Tell me her name. I *knew* it. You don't even think of her as a person, do you? You don't care about anybody but yourself. I should never have taken you back. *Never!*"

Indignant you think of Lars, how you played with him, invited him to dinner, the poor chubby, shy, fatherless kid. You are about to protest – *I care about Lars!* – but keep your mouth shut.

You drink your ouzos in silence, and silently, she rises from the balcony table and goes in to bed. You pour another. The moon is down low over the dark water, and you whisper for your own ears the remainder of the Seféris – "The stranger and the enemy/We have seen him in the mirror…" – wondering what you might see if your soul could ever gaze into itself. But of course, that is the poet's irony: It cannot. We cannot see ourselves, only one another. Occasionally perhaps we catch a reflected glimpse but it is a reflection in water, quickly dispersed in ripples that disappear again.

You understand then, that night alone on the balcony in Agios Nikolaos on Crete, that Liv and you will never find your way to one another. At best it will be a cold truce. You can only hold on as long as you can for the privilege of being near your children while they are still children.

What is it that happens to make a marriage go bad? you wonder. Your parents' marriage was not good either. Or perhaps it had been, at the start. You saw pictures of them at the beach when your brother and sister were children, and they all looked happy, so many years before you were born. But by the time you came along, by the time you were conscious of your surroundings, you realized that things were not good between them. But they stayed together for thirty-two years – until the day of Dad's death.

That kind of life, you had thought then, will never happen to me.

You pour another ouzo, add water, sip. You light a cigar and stare up into the black, star-scattered sky, and you understand that one day, you too will be judged by your children. They will shake their heads over you. *Mom and Dad*, they will say and shake their heads. *Mom and Dad*.

I AM JOE'S PROSTATE

The year is 1994. You are 50 years old. It is three domiciles and one wife ago. In the bathroom of your somewhat classy north Copenhagen bungalow, you stand over the porcelain and pee. You have not yet learned the word *micturate*. You are so innocent. Finished, you wash your hands and open the door, startled to find your wife of twenty years marriage listening there.

She says, "You piss like an old man." She is a physician. She says, "You need to have that checked. I'll make an appointment for you."

Three weeks later, you ride your classic, green, three-speed Raleigh twenty-five minutes north to G_____ Hospital. Through the maze of hallways without a thread or a clue as to what you are about to experience, you find the urology department. An extremely large First Resident with no name plate on the pocket of his white coat extends his extremely large hand of extremely large fingers and mumbles his name. His first name. Surnames here, you will learn, are not offered, delivered only begrudgingly upon explicit request.

With a file under his arm, Dr. Mumble leads you into an examination room, has you remove your pants and perch on your knees on a metal, paper-decked table. Without prelude or warning, he rams a long fat finger up your kazoo.

You bellow, then croak, "Is that supposed to hurt so much."

"It varies," he says absently, his back to you, washing his fingers at a sink, and continues, "There is a certain enlargement, but not more than might be expected for your age." You wonder what it is that has a certain enlargement. You finally, some years ago, learned about the existence of the clitoris, but still know nothing of the prostate. Dr. Mumble looks in the file – *your* file, instructs you to go to the nurses' station for further instructions. There you are given a large glass of colored water to drink and directed by a woman in white into a long narrow room where you are further instructed to micturate into an odd-looking steel vase with a slanted, recessed lid. Kindly, the woman in white steps out and shuts the door. You understand intuitively what micturate means, recognize it as the word of choice here in the land of white and yellow.

The odd-looking steel vase, however, does not look like something you would *want* to micturate in. Nonetheless, you do so. The slanted recessed lid flutters like a butterfly under your stream, causing a kind of needle on a machine you only just noticed to zigzag along a moving belt of graph paper. When the last few drops have dripped, causing the needle to twitch and fall still, you zip away that of you which most rarely sees the light of day and wonder what to do. You have no further instructions. Perhaps you should just go home. Yes, perhaps that is what you should do.

But the woman in white is waiting outside the door for you. You notice that she has beautiful eyes and very sensuous lips. You caution yourself not to occupy your imagination with such details in your current situation, and the woman in white with sensuous lips turns you over to another of her sort, though larger of build and darker of complexion. She leads you into another room and instructs you to undress. You have never been naked in front of a strange woman unless the object was hanky-panky.

Everything? you wonder, but trust she will say stop at the appropriate moment.

"You can leave your shirt on," she says with a smile, and you think of Joe Cocker and wonder if she is teasing you. There is no name tag at her breast pocket, and she has mumbled neither her name nor her rank. She pats an examination table, indicating that you are to lie there. Face up, you presume. You do as you are told, noting distantly how passive you have become.

She takes your penis in her fingers. *Your penis!* She sprays something into it. You say, "*Ow!*"

"Yes," she whispers and begins to stuff some manner of wire down your penis. You are rather amazed that such things go on so close to the civilized streets on which you until today so innocently dwelt. It reminds you of a scene in an Alfred Hitchcock film. *Frenzy.* It occurs to you that some men would no doubt pay a great deal of money to have a woman perform this kind of act and curse your imagination, turn your eyes away from her lips which are also rather sensual. You concentrate on not noticing the sensation of her fingers touching you, but anyway there seems no real danger that the jaunty head of Eros will poke up here.

She says, "Tell me when you feel the urge to micturate."

You felt the urge to micturate the instant she started stuffing that wire into you. Now you notice that the remainder of the wire is attached to another machine, the nature or function of which you are not destined to come to know.

You say, "Now, please."

She encourages you to stand before another metal vase and says, "You may micturate now."

Nothing happens.

She taps her foot.

Nothing happens.

She says, "Would you like me to wait outside?"

"Yes, please."

She withdraws. Still nothing happens.

When she returns she looks into the empty vase and sighs. "It would seem you didn't really have to micturate," she says.

"I thought I did."

She hums. "Well, we'll just have to try again."

It seems to you this would be an appropriate moment for her to stroke your hair and say, "You poor guy, you, it will all be over shortly, I promise," but instead she says, "Back on the table."

Having finally successfully micturated to her satisfaction, you anticipate release back into the world of clothing where private parts are truly private. Indeed, you are allowed to dress, but are then led into yet another room, instructed to lie on yet another table and left alone for a bit, perhaps to examine your conscience and feel guilty about the fact that you didn't really have to micturate before, but only said so to make her stop shoving that wire in. At length, two women come in, and you are instructed to open your pants. Why does this not surprise you? And why are you not surprised not to know their names or professions? You might ask, but there have been so many nameless people by now that it hardly seems to matter.

The taller, dark-haired of the two women seems to be in charge. She tugs your pants down to your pubis, applies some oil and lays a flat round metal thing the size of a small saucer on your pubic hair. She slides it around a bit. You notice she is looking not at you but at a screen alongside.

"Excellent," she says. "Your bladder is completely empty. Nothing is left. Excellent."

You ask, "May I go home now then?"

"Won't be long," she says. "Please wait here."

Presently another woman in white enters. "You'll have to take off all your clothes except your shirt," she says.

You wonder about your socks, but think, *Fuck it!* Back on the table, naked but for your unbuttoned shirt, and suddenly half a dozen people, men and women, tramp in and surround the table you are on. No one is identified, but a familiar face appears amidst them – that of the very large First Resident with very large fingers. All things considered, you are glad that you are lying on your back. To put you at ease, he peers down into your face with a terrifying smile and says, "I bet this won't be nearly as bad as you fear."

Then he is inserting a wand the thickness of three or four pencils into Private Johnson while he and the other unidentified people peer alternately at you, at a screen, at you, at a screen.

The wand seems to have been plunged into the very pit of your soul where it is being stirred around. You groan, but it elicits no attention or relief. You cross your arms and groan louder. Someone, a woman, tries to uncross your arms to pin your hands down which seems to you a very odd thing for her to want to do. You decide to make a stand. Your arms are crossed and will stay that way, and you set free all the groans within you, listening with some obtuse comfort to their melody, flooding from your chest in minor key.

The very large First Resident peers unsympathetically into your face and snaps, "Would you please *stop that!*"

But you and your groans are working together now, at last you have a partner and you will not let him go until that wand is removed from your inner sanctum.

When the thing is out, you lay groggily on the table. A woman in white hands you a pail. "You may have to micturate," she says.

How can I micturate when my bladder has just been pronounced excellently empty? you wonder, but micturate you do. It comes in pints and quarts. You note the level of micturition rising toward the lip of the pail and croak, "Nurse! Another bucket, *hurry*, please!"

At last, dressed again, dazed, you sit in a chair alongside a desk in an empty room, waiting. You do not know what you are waiting for. No doubt you have been told to wait. Thoughts of escape no longer find refuge in your consciousness. You wait. The door opens. The large First Resident appears with the same thin folder under his arm. *Your* folder.

He smiles at you. "Did you have a bad time of it?" he asks.

"It was no picnic lunch in the Tivoli Gardens," you say, but your bravado rings lame even in your own ears.

He sits, opens the file. "Okay," he says. "We can offer two forms of treatment. Surgical or pharmaceutical."

You don't even think to ask treatment for what. Instantly, you yelp, "Pharmaceutical, please." *No incisions.*

"Don't dismiss the surgical possibility," he says earnestly. "It is by far the fastest and most effective." He looks at you expectantly.

"I think I should prefer the pharmaceutical," you say.

"*Pre-cision*," he says, making a ring of finger and thumb and jolting it. "With surgical precision we can take the thinnest slice or two, thin as the thinnest salami slices, thinner. I urge you to consider it. It's safe and precise. I'm required to tell you about the possibility of side effects but the chances are *extremely* slight."

"Of…?"

"Uh, impotence. And incontinence. I am required to tell you that. But it is highly unlikely. Unlikely. With this procedure you won't have to be getting up two or three times in the middle of the night to urinate any more."

You say, "I don't get up in the middle of the night to urinate. Only like if I drink a bottle of beer at bedtime."

He furrows his brow, looks at the folder on his desk. "Here it says that you do."

"Well," you hear yourself say, "I am sitting right here and telling you that I don't. So what it says there is not correct."

The very large First Resident juts out his lower lip. He looks very sad. For reasons unknown, you thank him as you slip out the door.

The thirty minute bicycle ride to your office is not the most pleasant you have ever experienced. Each of the morning's invasions is echoed in every bump and pothole and curbstone that the rims of your Raleigh strike. At the office, your wife phones to ask how things went.

"Everything's fine," you say. "There was nothing wrong with me."

Epilogue

A dozen years, two domiciles, one wife, and no medical problems later, a routine blood test teaches you a new scrap of scientific terminology: PSA. The letters stand for Prostate Specific Antigen, but that sounds even more cruelly clinical than the simple, jaunty 'PSA.' You learn that PSA should not be higher than 4, but yours is 6.9. A follow-up sample shows it to be 12. By now you know what that very large First Resident was talking about slicing like a salami – your prostate. You might have known this sooner if only the *Reader's Digest* had included an article entitled "I am Joe's Prostate" in their talking organ series back in the '50s. But you know now how good your little walnut-sized prostate has been to you all these years, with what joy it has assisted.

Although you have no symptoms – no prostate enlargement, no urinary difficulties, no pain – the elevated PSA alarms your GP sufficiently to send you once again for tests – this time to F_____ Hospital. Here the personnel seem considerably more like human beings than they did at G_____ Hospital. They have names and identify themselves as doctors or nurses, and this time you are equipped with questions and a pad and pen. You write everything down. You are alert to the possibility that they may endeavor to insert foreign objects into narrow hypersensitive places, and you are determined not to allow them to do so. So determined are you that they measure your blood pressure at 160 over 120. But this time, they navigate another canal, through the backdoor with ultrasound needles. You are told that there will be some discomfort but no real pain.

There is terrific discomfort and real pain as well. Each time the doctor positions the needle and aims, watching the ultrasound screen, he says by way of warning, "And...*now!*" and something painfully uncomfortable happens somewhere you have never felt anything but pleasure before. You engage in a philosophical discourse with yourself as to the differentiation between discomfort and pain.

First, they take six biopsies. No cancer. Then they take thirteen more biopsies. No cancer. But your PSA has now risen to 15. They take twelve more biopsies. By now, after 31 biopsies, you are urinating and ejaculating blood, but still no cancer is found. Your PSA drops to 9, hops back to 12, up to 19, back down to 14, up to 18, down to 13, up to 20. Once your prostate has recovered from all the probing and sticking, you have no further signs of blood in your urine or seed.

But there is a tall, slender long-faced chief physician there at F_____ Hospital who knows, who *intuits*, that the cancer is there. He reminds you of the policeman Porfiry Petrovitch in *Crime & Punishment.* Or a taller, morose version of Lt. Colombo of the LAPD. They have not yet found it but it *is* there he assures you. He is, in fact, eighty percent sure it is there and fifteen percent sure that it has already spread. But he can do nothing until he has the hard evidence: a cancer cell. He wants to take a scrape of your prostate. He wants to put you into full narcosis (there where they stop your heart and lungs for a while and keep you alive by the grace of a machine) and scrape the tiny five percent portion of your prostate where the ultrasound needles can't reach. Then you will come out of narcosis, and he will send the tissue sample to the pathologists for determination of whether there are malignant cells present.

Your ex-wife was a pathologist. She once revealed to you how difficult it is to determine malignancy. Sometimes healthy cells are falsely identified as malignant. Sometimes malignant cells are falsely identified as healthy. She quit practicing because the hospital administration was pressuring her to make too many fast decisions about what was and was not malignant.

This long-faced morose physician who is convinced that cancer is present in your prostate, which has otherwise been so good to you for half a century, will then, once he has found the cancer, be able to make a diagnosis and offer treatment. The treatment he urges will be removal of the prostate. All of it.

"You're fortunate," he tells you. "You're still young, and the cancer is very early. You can be completely cured."

Of the cancer that might not be there. Any possible side effects?

"There is a risk, I am obliged to tell you, that the scrape could result in impotence and/or incontinence."

And removal of the prostate?

"That *will* lead to impotence and incontinence. But the worst likely side-effect of the scrape, which is not very likely to occur at all, although I am obliged to inform you of the slight possibility, would be a modest leakage and a possible reversal of your ejaculatory trajectory."

You stare at his long, morose face, his protruding eyes, and you are aware that your own face radiates the meaning of the word *aghast*. "*What, exactly,*" you whisper, "does that mean?"

"Well, when you have sex, which you could continue to have quite satisfactorily by the way, you might be likely to ejaculate into your bladder instead of, well...outward. But the pleasure would be precisely the same, the sensation."

Incredulously, you tell him, "The pleasure would *not* be the same at all. The whole point of ejaculating is to do it into someone else! You think I'd be happy fucking my own bladder!" For one disoriented moment, you picture *impregnating* your own bladder.

"No need to be facetious," he quietly advises you. "Besides this is all quite hypothetical." His expression clearly is one he learned in a patient management course: Deactivating the Prostate-Protection Reflex in the Recalcitrant Aging Male Patient.

You are invited into another room to watch a video entitled, *Grand Dad's Prostate Cancer.* In it, a man who has had his prostate removed plays with his two very cute grandchildren, a boy and a girl, twins of about four. He sports a wispy grey beard and has very tiny teeth; he looks into the camera and smiles a rather silly smile with his tiny white teeth. "My grandchildren think it is very funny that they have just *stopped* wearing diapers and Grand Dad has to *start* wearing them again." He chuckles.

You are not amused. You definitely do not want to wear diapers. And not that you're such a stud or anything, but you do greatly enjoy waking each morning with some lead in your pencil as indeed you cherish the occasional two-backed beast with your beloved or even the good old honeymoon of the hand. You definitely do not wish to take a permanent vacation to the land where even Viagra offers no hope. You will never willingly ejaculate into your own bladder – which seems to you of a magnitude of strangeness equal to the man in the Ripley's Believe It Or Not, Volume 2, Sexual Abberations, who inserted a 75 watt lightbulb into his own colon.

You develop your own future plan of treatment. You will return to the lake. On the east side of Copenhagen there is a lake you love. You love this lake because it is a street lake, in the midst of the bustling city. You have loved this lake from the moment you first spied it, thirty-four years ago. It is called Black Dam Lake, and there is an old Copenhagen proverb: *I'll go out to Black Dam Lake.*

If and when it should become necessary, on a fair and sunny day, you will rent a row boat from the rental wharf on Black Dam Lake. You will paddle out to the center of the lake, and there you will drop anchor. You will unpack the picnic lunch you will have brought with you in a wicker basket. You will dine on smoked eel and dark rye bread spread with raw fat. Lots of it. And because fish must swim, you will drink cold bottles of beer. Many of them. And iced snaps in your favorite Holmgaard aquavit glass, many of them. While you dine, you will watch the swans float past like beautiful white question marks. You will watch the ducks and glebes paddle along the surface, and to encourage the seagulls – for they are an important part of your plan – you will fling bits of bread and eel up into the air to get them hovering overhead in an excited, crying cluster.

And then, when you are sufficiently satisfied, sufficiently besotted but not yet incapacitated, you will take the pistol from your belt, place the barrel in your mouth, pointed upwards toward your cranial cavity and pull the trigger. It will be a high caliber pistol and will tear a broad path through your brain, spraying bits and clumps of grey matter upward, which the seagulls will catch in their beaks and gobble down, wheeling over the lake, their gullets full of morsels of your thought and personality so that you will sweep across the lake like a great pointillist consciousness on your way to forever.

Where will you get a pistol?

Oh, you'll get one. By Charlton Heston's eyes, you will!

And how can you be sure you'll be strong and deliberate enough to carry all this through when that day comes.

Well, isn't it pretty to think you might?

Coda

Nonetheless, once again, you sit in a chair before the desk of Porfiry Petrovitch.

"You must choose now," he says. "The number is very high. The disease is present. It may already have spread. I *know* this."

His protruding eyes make you think of the face in an ancient ikon.

You say, "Well, I had a second opinion from …"

"I *know* the source of your second opinion," says Porfiry Petrovitch, "both professionally and socially. He is a nice fellow and a good internist, but he is *not* a urological surgeon, and he knows *nothing* of this."

Porfiry Petrovitch is younger than you, but his eyes are stronger, his protruding eyes. You turn your own gaze from them, look out the window behind him at the slate gray sky, toward the door which is shut and unpromising. His protruding eyes never waver from your face. They contain the words that he has spoken, that he need not repeat: "You must choose now." But he has already chosen.

So you nod. The procedure is scheduled. For three weeks you watch its inexorable approach. Then, finally, in the ward, you are dressed in a flimsy gown, being measured for support stockings, checked over like an old car, stuck with needles, thermometers, fed a pill and told it is best you get into bed because you might get woozy.

You note that you feel pretty good. Feisty even. Planning some havoc as a silent orderly rolls your bed out into the hall, the elevator up to the OR where the anesthesiologist looks soberly into your eyes and says, "We have to ask your name, standard procedure."

"My name," you say, "is Porfiry Petrovitch," giving the name of the head of the urology unit. The surgeon, alongside, laughs. "Then we'll cut right in!"

A nurse adjusts the valve set into the vein on back of your hand and the anesthesiologist does something to it, and now you are feeling *very* good. You cannot believe it is possible to feel this good.

"Think about something nice now," the anesthesiologist says.

You say, "I feel pretty damn good," and he whispers at your ear, "Men pay lots of money to feel the way you're feeling right now."

You do not reply. You are completely absorbed thinking about your wife, about how she looked in her aquamarine two-piece swim suit last summer on the beach at Skorpios, the surf frothing around her beautiful legs, blond, tan, smiling. She is smiling for you with her blue blue eyes, drawing you forward into her gaze, her gorgeous body…

Suddenly they're rolling you out again.

"Say, where are you taking me?" Your voice sounds slurry.

"It's over," says a nurse. "We want you down in the wake-up room for a while where we can keep an eye on you."

You open your mouth and hear yourself say, "Dr. No. Ursula Andress." This seems hilarious to you, but no one even smiles. Can they even hear you? Are you dead? Is this death? You want to explain your words but you notice a fly on the sheet, just sitting there, so still.

A while later you notice that you are hooked up to some contraption on which hangs a clear plastic bag of blood. From the bag runs a tube which disappears under your sheet. You become aware of a very annoying discomfort in the worst of places. The blood, you understand then, is your own micturition. You have been fitted with a catheter. You are given permission to get out of bed. You do so carefully, supporting yourself on the contraption from which your bag of blood hangs and to which you are connected by a long flexible tube. The contraption looks like some kind of garment rack, and you discover that it is on wheels.

For want of anything better to do, you shuffle out of the room and along the ward corridor, rolling the rattling contraption alongside you, your bag of blood swaying there. You do not like looking at the bag of blood, but it seems wherever you send your eyes, they always wander back to it, recoiling from it again, wandering back. You shuffle the length of the hall, learn how to turn your contraption without causing the connecting tube to tug at your exhausted tugger where you least want to be tugged just now. It occurs to you that all the nurses here are very good-looking, and you advise yourself not to even think about that for a second lest your tugger begin to get untoward ideas.

You begin to shuffle again, back along the corridor. Three men sit around a table, their contraptions parked alongside them as they play cards with a greasy-looking deck. "How come you don't sit down?" one of them asks as you shuffle past.

"Hurts less when I'm on my feet."

"Hurts less when he's on his feet," another man explains to the first as you proceed to shuffle the night away.

Next morning the surgeon comes in to visit. Not Porfiry Petrovitch but the smiling good-humored fellow who actually did the cutting. "Just to let you know," he says brightly, "that I took three good slices and everything looked fine. No enlargement, no irregularity. It is a good-looking prostate I saw."

"Should be," you say. "It's Joe's prostate."

They laugh as though they understand.

The surgeon returns that afternoon, a nurse alongside him, a dark-haired nurse who fills her translucent white uniform so perfectly that you have to avert your eyes for fear of losing your catheter.

"Is there still blood in his urine?" the surgeon asks her.

"The color of rosé wine," she replies.

You thank her for ensuring that you will never again for the remainder of your life drink rosé wine.

"We don't drink rosé wine here either," she says with a twinkle of regret.

"How do you feel about going home now?" the smiling surgeon asks.

Then you are alone with the nurse. You are in bed. She is alongside. She reaches under the covers. Could this be love? you wonder as she whispers, "Take a deep breath now. I'm going to remove the catheter. I'm afraid I'll have to move back your foreskin first."

"If you try to do that," you say, "we'll be here forever because I don't have one."

"Then take a breath."

You do, and you hear a strangling gargling horror-comic groan contract your throat: *Aargh*! You consider that the first person who ever thought to write that sound with just those letters had been through this very procedure.

She holds it up for you to see – a thick pencil-like device with a ragged bulb on the end. She points at the bloody bulb. "That's the thing that hurts coming out."

You have just reached an understanding of what the ugliest word in the language is: *Catheter*. Three syllables of misery. Even worse in Danish: *Kateter*.

It will be a fortnight before you have the biopsy results. That, you know, is when the treatment can begin. The aim of this exercise has been to tenderize you for the real cut.

Two weeks ensue with frequent, fiery micturitions. You live in dread of the micturition urge. You have twisted the water pipe alongside your jakes into a pretzel and ground a millimeter off your molars. You sustain yourself by contemplating your hatred of the word "catheter." You check its etymology, hoping that it is named for its inventor so that you can put a face on your hatred, but find it is built of Greek and Latin word parts that mean something like "passing through." Every time you grit your teeth and micturate fire you consider the fact that this ugly collection of letters – some of your favorite letters of the alphabet, too, though here organized in the ugliest possible fashion – represents a device which threatens to become a long-term fixture in your life.

There will be catheters, there will be catheters… In the room the nurses come and go talking of catheters… We have lingered by the catheters of the sea by sea girls wreathed in plastic tubing… I should have been a pair of ragged catheters scuttling across the floors of rosé-colored seas.

On the appointed day, you enter the appointed consultation room and shake the hand of the smiling surgeon as well as the hand of the dark-haired nurse at his side. The dark-haired lady. There is always a dark-haired lady. Saying, "Take a deep breath now…"

You are motioned to a chair. The smiling surgeon sits, lays the flat of his palm on a folder before him on the desk top. "Well," he says, and smiles. "Nothing. There is nothing."

"Nothing?"

"No cancer. Not even a single cell. I took samples from every corner where the ultra sound needles can't reach. And there is nothing. You have a healthy prostate."

"What happened?"

"Sometimes the PSA is wrong," he says. The dark-haired nurses nods, smiles reassuringly. "Sometimes the PSA is wrong."

Thus, after two years, twenty blood tests, thirty-four biopsies, the last three of which were surgical, and two weeks of micturating fire, you are sent out into the world, onto the sunny pavement to find your way in a world of health.

What is a man to do?

Down the street and on the other side, you see a sign that says BAR. You head for it.

ADVENTURES OF AN OLD DUDE

Bodil, the woman you've lived with for fifteen years, asks if you will have time within the next week or so to listen to a few things she would like to talk about. You are sitting on one of the plush sofas in the high-ceilinged living room of your rent-controlled apartment – her apartment technically – your wall of bookcases behind you, alternately gazing out the tall windows over the broad, bright boulevard and editing the manuscript of the novel that's just earned you a lucrative contract – things finally beginning to turn your way, albeit at an advanced age.

What about right now? you suggest.

Are you sure? she asks. I'm not disturbing you?

You could avoid this, but your curiosity has the better of you. Something has been working behind her baby-blues of late. You want to get this out of the way so you can get on with your novel. Also, her analyst, Alphonse, who has taken to hanging around rather often of late and involving himself in your conversations is not here at the moment.

No, really, you say. What better time than now?

She goes to her desk and opens the drawer, removes a notebook. She sits in the armchair opposite you on the sofa, and you don't like the awkward way she hunches over the notebook. She is nervous about what she is going to say, and suddenly you realize that something is coming that you are not prepared for. She opens the pad, runs her finger down the page while you observe her hair, which would be grey if it weren't blond, her face which is still attractive though handled by time, her body now round at the middle but the body you love.

One red-pointed fingernail stops at a line and taps. She looks up at you. With breathy resignation, she says, Yeah. Then begins.

And suddenly you are without a woman, living elsewhere, in cramped quarters, beneath low ceilings, behind windows that look out on a ground-floor bicycle rack, your books stacked two rows deep in half as many bookcases as you are accustomed to, no room for your dining table that seated twelve. Anyway, with your new appliances, if you try to make dinner for more than one, your electrical system blows, as you learned on Thanksgiving Day when your son and daughter came over and the three of you wound up in total darkness with a half-cooked turkey in the oven, pots of half-boiled potatoes and yams and peas on the electric stove-top just as the turkey pan should have been raked for the gravy.

You did not expect this.

You did not expect that she would be sending you and others strange, vaguely poisonous letters.

You did not expect to dine alone on Christmas Eve on pork belly and chopped cabbage in an upscale diner by the harbor, the only restaurant in the city serving on this holy night, at a one-man table amidst a scattering of commercial travelers stranded for the holiday in a foreign port. You did not expect to spend New Year's Eve sulking over your champagne and marzipan cake or New Year's Day alone in your pajamas watching *Quo Vadis* on TCN.

People pose indiscreet questions. The woman who cuts your hair – who also "does" Bodil's – asks boldly, What in the world happened?

Happened?

Between the two of you?

Well, you say, I don't think I'd like to discuss that.

Well *you* left *her* anyway. Always easier for the one who leaves. Left her explosively! Bodil told me. One day to the next. So I guess it's easier for you. What happened anyway?

Well, you say, I don't think I'd like to discuss that.

The haircutter nudges your shoulder with her slinky hip. So you're free now, ey? Maybe I should start playing matchmaker?

Well, you say, I don't think I'd like to discuss that, but you wonder who she might have in mind.

Motion, you have been told, is important so you rise two or three times a week at six-fifteen and, before breakfast, trudge three blocks in Nordic winter dark to the fitness center where you plunge into the insufficiently heated pool to swim a kilometer, counting laps to blank your thoughts, in the hated element immersed, thankful when you have the pool to yourself so you do not have to take evasive action to avoid the intrusion of splashers or erratic lane shifters or heedless back strokers who might whack you on the snout. Reach and scoop water, reach and scoop and paddle the legs in your own self-styled slow-motion crawl, fifty lengths in as many minutes before breaching out of the pool to do some stretching on the wet tiles to avoid leg and back cramps and, feeling virtuous, jog down the stairs to the men's locker to strip for the shower.

One day outside the shower room two naked younger men with whom you have a nodding acquaintance look strangely at you, eyes large, mouths open, as though they are seeing a ghost.

Finally one of the two, fashionably bald with a lot of black hair on his naked body, says, Good thing you're not dead. The other adds, Good thing it wasn't you who drowned.

Someone drowned? you say.

Old guy. Sank like a stone. Stroke maybe. Bottom of the pool. Lucky another guy was there, strong swimmer, dove right in and got him up out of the water. He was dead.

He was dead?

Dead, yeah.

The showers within are splashing as you attempt to ingest this information.

So, how was it lucky?

The bald hairy one says, This guy knew first aid and resuscitated him. Weird. To be dead. And then alive again. We didn't know who it was. They carried him out on a stretcher.

They look at one another, back at you, and the one says, We thought it was you. You usually swim at that time. He was an old guy. Seventy.

You say, I'm sixty-four.

Still. Thought it was. Good thing it wasn't.

Outside on the street, you stop to gaze through the wall of windows at the big pool, its surface still and glassy, no one in the water. Behind the tall broad window, beneath the high spotlight-speckled ceiling, the tiled floor empty in the dim light, water reflecting the color of the aquamarine pool bottom. The big empty space looks like something from a David Lynch film – menacing in its stillness, lifeless matter that somehow might absorb and smother any vitality in its proximity, ready to absorb more – like if you looked too long, it might suck you right in and swallow you.

―――――

Later that afternoon passing the Blue Dog Café, wrapped about in dazed wonderings, you see a former student stepping out the café door into the street – tall and slender with startlingly blue eyes and long gleaming black hair and a pretty, mischievous smile. She is wearing a blue silk scarf over the gleaming cascade of her black hair, and you say, I really have to tell you: That scarf looks so beautiful against your hair.

She reaches a long-fingered hand to touch your arm, says, I hear you left your wife.

You see no reason to specify that she was, in fact, *not* your wife or that *she*, in fact, kicked *you* out. It is no one's business even if your ex-woman is spreading the word that you left her.

You say, We've parted, yes.

Her pretty eyes sparkle mischievously. So you're free now?

You chuckle. She is standing so close that you can feel the warmth of her body even through her elegant long grey woolen coat. You have not been alone for thirty-five years. You were with your actual wife for twenty years and almost immediately after that you took up with Bodil. Are you really going to do this again? Could it be this easy? No, what are you thinking? This girl is half your age, less than half. She's not even thirty. You're an old man to her.

You nod toward the door of the café she has just left, ask, Shall we have a coffee?

A euphemism. She has a cosmopolitan and you have a double vodka on the rocks. She sits close beside you at the table, her hand on your forearm, her drink quickly empty. She picks up your expensive soft elk-skin gloves and draws them slowly, sensuously onto her long-fingered hands, smiling that mischievous smile which combines with the contrast of blue eyes and black hair to take your breath away. You avoid remembering the gloves were a gift from Bodil on your last birthday – your sixty-fourth. You order another round of drinks. Unlikely as it may be, it seems you are about to get lucky, very lucky. You wonder if this could be true, try to review the parameters of the situation to be certain you are reading the signs correctly. But no mistaking the mischief in that smile. Then it occurs to you that she is a bit tipsy, must have been drinking before you met her on the street, maybe smoking pot, doing coke, who knows what young people do today. Might even be worse than you were, than you are, but no, this is a sweet young woman, and she is gazing into your eyes. Involuntarily you recall once again that, in fact, she is not yet thirty. In fact, she might not even be twenty-five. She might not even be quite aware of what that gaze is doing to your recently damaged maleness.

What, uhm, are we doing? you ask.

Doing? she says.

You are a very attractive woman. It almost feels as though we are making moves that will lead us to bed.

Oh, no! she says quietly. That's not what I meant.

You wonder if she is consciously paraphrasing Prufrock. For if she is consciously paraphrasing Prufrock that adds an unpleasant edge of irony to your embarrassment that you did not manage to sail more smoothly through this, acting like an adult as you might have been expected to do.

You brave a self-ironic smile, say, I have seen the moment of my greatness flicker. You do not mention perfume from a dress or the singing mermaids.

―――――――

You get to know your new upstairs neighbors. Through the ceiling, you hear the woman upstairs neighbor saying to the man upstairs neighbor, You're starting that bullshit again, are you?

His response is a mutter, but you can guess what he said for she then says, I don't give a fuck if everyone hears. I don't give a fuck. You know what? Want to know something? Nobody likes you. It's true. They don't. Nobody. Likes. You.

There is the sound of footsteps, the sound of a door, more footsteps on the staircase. You peek out the window, over the bicycle rack see the upstairs man neighbor get into his car and drive off.

You sit on the sofa, lower your face into your palms. Then you reach for the remote, click the reruns channel.

An extended winter of discontent follows, with regular bouts of the sickness unto death and dark nights of the soul, alone, in the company of your Black Dog, hunched before flat-screen reruns of *Fraser* and *Friends*, at one point actually beginning to care about the plights of the "people" depicted, Dad and Niles and Daphne, Joey, Rachel, Monica, Phoebe, Chandler, Ross, though you mix up their names, as though they are two groups of people you know who frequent the same café, chuckling at their jokes and situations, falling for Dr. Crane's assistant, Roz, who is always looking for a mate, getting aroused every time the dark-haired pretty one who used to be fat but is now svelte comes on the screen in *Friends*, vacillating in your feelings about Rachel and Phoebe, although you definitely would not kick them out of the sack, but also coming to your senses every so often in the midst of all this with a fear that you might have gotten careless with your PIN codes in those days when Bodil was the love of your life and you of hers.

After some weeks of this, you notice that your upstairs neighbors seem to have parted. There are no further arguments or accusations coming down through the ceiling. You wonder if anybody likes you, decide that somebody somewhere might at least find you not disagreeable.

You decide that you do not mind being alone and no longer go for the remote while you chew your evening ham-and-cheese sandwich with Dijon or fried porkchop and red cabbage or steak and salad with balsamico and flute and glass of cab. You begin to refrain from taking solace in the fact that, in any event, the reaper will soon be at your door, begin to speculate that you may even have a good ten, even twenty or more years remaining, look at the actuarial tables, sixty-five percent of men alive at sixty-five will live to ninety-five – or was it thirty-five percent will live to eighty-five? No matter, you still potentially have roughly half of an early twentieth-century life expectancy remaining.

This makes you begin to feel if not good, at least not so bad. But then your hibernating libido rears its puckish head anew, and you begin wondering what your chances might be of getting lucky in the old hanky-panky department. It had been quite some time since you and Bodil engaged in even the lawful hanky-panky of cohabitation. You wonder if you have forgotten how. You did come close to it with a cute colleague at a literary conference a few months before the break-up, but decided that would be unkind and unfair to Bodil who was home alone, trusting you to behave yourself. On the other hand, Bodil had already at that time begun conferring rather frequently with her analyst named, of all things, Alphonse, who, she said, had told her he learned as much from her as she from him so did not even charge her a fee. He had begun hanging around the apartment about then, too. Might *she* have been hanky-pankying *him* while you were denying yourself the cute colleague?

Then you remember that, in fact, you and Bodil had had hanky-panky together while you were still married to your wife and Bodil was still married to her second husband. That had always seemed to you a circumstance of extreme coincidence – indeed, an exceptional case occasioned by exceptional marital dysfunction resulting in extreme and understandable horniness. But now it re-opens a question which has always puzzled you: Do people, in fact, freely and indiscriminately allow themselves to hanky-panky others even when they are married or otherwise cohabiting? Are people really so despicable? What is the real status of this hanky-panky business? Okay, it is true that you have had hanky-panky enough in your lifetime, but at least you had the decency to feel guilty about it if it happened when you were married or cohabiting or even just going steady.

Frankly, you don't even know if you actually want any hanky-panky now. But perhaps you should give it a try just to find out.

You go out on "dates." Are they really dates? What exactly is a date anyway? You meet a woman in a bookshop, an artist, perhaps ten years younger than yourself, very smartly dressed and, in fact, handling one of your own books. The clerk, a young woman for whom you have always had a soft spot, says to her, Are you aware that the author of that book is standing right behind you?

There is surprise, laughter, shoulder shrugging, brow touching. You chat, get her number, invite her for lunch over which you learn she has just come unhappily out of a long-term affair. You murmur that that can take some time to get over.

Years, she says.

You say, Well I don't know about *years*. Months perhaps.

She has refused the cremant you suggested, prefers an orange smoothie.

But you go ahead, she says.

You notice there is something about her voice and the tip of her nose that repels you. Are you so shallow as to be repelled by a voice and the tip of a nose? you wonder. But there is no denying that this woman does not interest you or that she is not interested in you either. Years, indeed! You're ready – what's wrong with *her*?! Does she think her love was so much greater than yours? That you're shallow?

Friday night you decide to go over to Christiania to hear jazz, ride the Metro underground, enter the third-world darkness of this walled squatter's city within the city of Copenhagen. The dark and rutted frozen mud streets are agreeable to your mood.

There are no signs on the clubs here, just old low dark brick buildings. You follow a side path to a door and find yourself in a building with a vast skate-board pit. You watch a young, hooded skate-boarder gracefully negotiating the steep slant of the wood walls, down up, hop and twist, down up, hop and twist and fall. He hits the wall, skateboard clattering, slides on his back down to the nadir of the pit, leaps to his feet and, skate board beneath his arm, climbs to the top again.

Wondering whether this is a metaphor, you withdraw, find your way by hit and miss to the Christiania Jazzklub where you buy a red-labeled Christiania pilsner, chug it down while the band blows a heart-probing rendition of "Night in Tunisia," and a friendly man beside you at the bar passes you a joint, which you toke before ordering another beer.

It is big band night, thirteen instruments, mostly brass and reeds, half a dozen different kinds of saxophone now blowing "Round Midnight." The baritone is being played by a tall, slender woman with long blond hair and thick black eyebrows; she stands holding the long instrument close in to her long body, the horn curving out from between her tightly blue-jeaned thighs. You recall hearing somewhere that a man should play the instrument of a woman's body like a fine violin. You wonder what it might be like to have your own body played by this woman like a baritone sax. Then you think the blood might rush uncomfortably to your head.

You entertain yourself during a pause in the music thinking about the man who invented the saxophone, a Belgian by the name of Antoine Sax, then that name makes you think of Alphonse the analyst who is perhaps at this moment cheering your ex-sweetheart and you wonder if you are intentionally trying to torment yourself.

You sit beside a woman of indeterminate age wearing bright red boots from which emerge long, attractive, black-stockinged legs. Although she is seated, you determine that she is taller than you. Not a problem for you, but some women want men to be taller than themselves. You sit up straight in your chair, take out your tin packet of mini-cigars, extend it to her. She accepts one. This seems a good sign. You light it for her. She drags, says, "Good." You say, Danish fashion, "Not the worst." She has an agreeable voice. A voice you could definitely fall for. And an unusual face. You keep stealing glances at her face to determine what precisely constitutes its unusualness. It is a strong but not unfeminine face. She nods toward an Indian woman sitting a few seats away, says, "See that woman? I was in India with her twenty-seven years ago when I was eighteen. But she doesn't remember me."

You are quick at arithmetic, even after a couple of beers and one toke, calculate that she is forty-five, redo the calculation to be certain. Yes, forty-five. You think about asking if she has ever considered the advantages of love with an older, shorter man, but caution yourself not to chance seeming flip. Perhaps you should find a coded manner in which to help her determine your own age, perhaps trimming off five or six years,. She asks if you are American, providing the perfect opportunity. You tell her, yes, but that you have been living in Copenhagen for thirty years, since you were twenty-eight. That's an easy calculation and only a mildly precautionary lie. You ask what she does. She tells you that she is a cemetery tour guide. You are aware that your mouth is open while trying to decide what you can possibly say to that. Is she jamming your head?

You say, What, like, you are some kind of real estate purveyor for people who want to be buried?

She laughs. She has a nice laugh. You could definitely fall for that laugh but advise yourself not to fall for anything until you have cleared up this matter of being a cemetery guide.

From a dainty pink back-pack, she removes a card which she extends to you. It shows the name of a tour guide bureau specializing in cemeteries and cemetery sculpture. She says that she takes groups around on walking tours of various cemeteries, gives talks on who is buried where. You know, she says, the graves of the famous.

Your alarm decelerates. You pocket the card, then realize you forgot to look at her name on it. You will do so discreetly in a few moments. You are ready for another beer and ask if she would like one. She would. Another good sign.

As you thread through the jumble of agreeably motley mismatched tables and chairs to the attractively dilapidated bar, the music starts up again – a good, belting brass rendition of "Love for Sale." As you wait for the bartender to uncap your beer bottles, the friendly man at the bar passes you a joint which you toke, then toke again and feel the top of your head snuggling up to the ceiling as you bury the smoke deep in your lungs, cough, and say, Good shit, as you pass it back. The evening seems to be going well.

When you return to the cemetery guide, realizing that you have forgotten to discreetly check her card for her name, and hand her one of the bottles of Christiania red-label beer, she asks whether you know the name of the number that is playing. You tell her "Love for Sale," then wonder if her getting you to say that title is significant, realize that you have perhaps already had one beer and two tokes too many, which is a pity because you are definitely interested in this woman with the attractive voice and laugh and long legs and unusual face and would like to determine whether you really stand a chance, but caution yourself not to risk revealing the state of your intoxication.

"Big Band Samba" is playing, all baker's dozen of brass and reeds blazing to fill the little club with sound. You are dancing in your chair. In a lull at the end of the number, you say to the woman, "I will soon have to withdraw because I have an early day tomorrow. But I would definitely like to stay in touch with you."

Her nod is pleasant but noncommittal. You clasp her hand in parting and gaze for a moment into her eyes, trying not to make the moment so significant as to alarm her, and you are out the door without mishap. Outside in the cold, you dig your handkerchief from your pocket and blow your nose as you walk the frozen-rutted mud paths to the street which is dark and empty as a Hopper woodcut. On the avenue, you wave down a taxi and watch the midnight streets roll past on either side, the short bridge into the center, across the King's New Square, along the long dark avenue to the east side, thinking back over the slightly surrealistic details of the night – with an unusual-faced cemetery guide. This is shit that you would never be able to imagine, you think, life being, as they say, stranger than fiction.

At home, you wonder, as you occasionally do, whether life in fact is some strange drama staged by superior beings for their amusement with the players having been hypnotized or drugged or simply bewitched into a state of semi-conciousness so that they think life is real while all the time it is merely staged, and you yourself are being manipulated among shadows and human metaphors. You think about the woman asking the title of that number and your answering "Love for Sale" and how for a dizzy second you wondered if that had been staged by her, but it might also have been staged by superior creatures, *les auteurs des choses*, who provided her with that line of dialogue, who arranged to have that number playing at just that point where she could exercise the line of dialogue in order to alert you to the possibility that she was indicating she would make her body available to you in exchange for cash.

You know, in fact, that some women in this country occasionally do just that if they run short of money at rent time. But why would the authors of this drama then have made her at the same time a cemetery guide? Could that have been a MacGuffin?

You realize abruptly that you are way drunker than you knew although there is a clarity to these thoughts, as though you are seeing through the seams of the drama that has been written for you to play in, an instant of near lucidity over which perhaps *les auteurs des choses* have no control – or perhaps this is simply another refinement of the drama they have written you into.

You advise yourself that this is completely crazy shit, wondering what might have been in that friendly stranger's casually passed joint, and rise from the sofa to check through your pockets for the card she gave you. In the pocket where you thought you had put it is only your dirty handkerchief. You check all your other pockets – jacket, shirt, overcoat. No card. Then you remember digging out your handkerchief to blow your nose just outside the club. The card could only have fluttered out then, fallen to the muddy ground right outside the door of the jazz club. Perhaps she would even see it as she left, think that you had purposely thrown it there to insult her, to indicate that she didn't mean shit to you.

You pace back and forth on the plank floor, holding your forehead, muttering curses at your own stupidity.

The next day is spent in hiding, eating unhealthy things, swilling sugar-free cola. At one point you try to google cemetery tours but find nothing of promise, google some porn instead but find it unimaginative and dispiriting.

By Sunday you are slept out, and your system seems to have sufficiently shed the poisons of paranoiac madness that you are ready to step out into the bright, cold world again.

You decide upon something sedate, a museum visit perhaps. The Hirschprung Collection on Stockholm Street, outside of which is a sculpture of an equestrian barbarian with three decapitated skulls dangling from his saddle. You study the gaping-mouthed heads, the proud anti-humanistic visage and posture of the barbarian upon his bulky stead, his short muscular body. You think of Cavafy's poem, "Waiting for the Barbarians," its despair that the barbarians might not be coming back, that there might not be any more barbarians, his anguished (or ironic) question – what will we do without the barbarians? You think of the Barbarian Bar over on the west side, but pay your four dollar admission and enter the little museum funded by the cigars you smoke.

As you stand gazing at the evocative light and shadows of a Hammershøj depicting an angular woman with no face in the corner of a room, a woman beside you admires your beret. You tell her you bought it in Paris. She has a nice smile. You chat, invite her for coffee. A euphemism, you thought, but she really does order coffee while you shamelessly ask for a pint of Hof, explaining to her that Hof in fact, like your Hirschsprung cigarillos, support the arts.

Do you smoke, too? she asks, tilting her head, then looks at the golden gleaming pint glass, looks at you, doles out the tiniest of smiles, says, "I need more sweetener." You steal a glance at her when she steps over to the counter for another packet of sugar. You try to imagine her somewhat short somewhat bulky body without clothes. Probably not much worse than your own body without clothes, but at least you don't have to look at your own body. What are you thinking? Pig! Isn't she a little too old for you anyway? How old is she? How old are you? Perhaps that is the question. Are you, like, an old man now? This is all so pointless anyway. In any event there is something about her eyes which begins to put you off. Some potentially brutal, even barbaric look about them. You picture her a-mount a bulky stead, your own gaping-mouthed head danging from her saddle, beret jammed down around your ears. You decide not to see her again.

Long winter days pass. In a café you are startled to read on the daily paper's culture pages that the former Danish ballet director Flemming Flindt is dead at 72. You and your first wife, then fiancée, saw him dance naked with his wife Vivi in *Death's*

Triumph in 1972. To this day you have a framed still photograph of Vivi's gorgeous butt in its prime hanging on your bedroom wall. It always cheers you up to gaze upon it. Disturbed at the thought that even the choreographer of *Death's Triumph* has been trumped by death at the age of 72 which is the new 52, you look around for someone to share this unhappy news with, notice a younger woman at the table beside you, reading a novel you greatly admire, Camus's *The Stranger*. You fold shut the newspaper with the scene of Flemming and Vivi dancing naked to the triumph of death and tell the young woman – who probably had not even yet been born at the time of that dance – that this café in fact is on the bank of the Copenhagen street lake on which Kierkegaard lived just over a century and a half before. She does not seem to comprehend why you would mention this so you explain the direct connection between Camus's *The Stranger* and Kierkegaard's leap of faith.

Her eyes open wide. She says, Oh! That might explain it. She tells you she was searching through *The Stranger* because it is referred to by a British rap group called Leap of Despair.

No, you say, Leap of faith, and she gives you a look of pity, perhaps directed at your unhipness, but what you are thinking is that her breasts, in fact, make you want to leap for joy. You chat. She is only 36, slender, darkly attractive. More than a quarter century younger than yourself. You remind yourself that you are sixty-four. Sometimes, because you do not so often have to see your own face, you forget that it is ageing. But isn't sixty-four the new forty-six? Would that make thirty-six the new sixteen? She asks if you are in a relationship, which seems a promising question. You tell her your relationship ended a few months ago.

Are you looking for another relationship? she asks.

I can't imagine not having another relationship, you say. With a woman, you add and wonder why you added that.

She shrugs. Well you could be gay if you want. We are what we are.

Absolutely. But I'm not gay. I've never been gay.

She smiles. Never say never, she says, experiment keeps people young. Then she adds, I didn't think you were anyway.

You exchange email addresses, trade a few brief innocent messages over the next few days. Then you don't hear from her for two weeks, following which she writes to invite you to meet her in a night café on the west side where the music starts at nine. I think you'll like it there, she says.

What does she mean by that? you wonder. Has she decided that you need to be taken out and shown places you might like? Does she think you're incapable of finding places you like on your own? Does she think you're a clueless old dude who needs help?

On the appointed day, the buses are on strike so you take the city train to the central station and have to walk the last mile, all the while wondering what might come of this, if anything. Will she be interested in hanky-panky? If so, will you be up for it? Since that last biopsy on your prostate, your apparatus has not been functioning optimally. You can get it up all right, but something funny happens now when you climax. You do get excited, and you do climax, but it is just not as thrilling as it was before the biopsy. Then you think that perhaps a 36-year-old woman would be more thrilling than your sixty-four year old hand.

In the café, she is waiting at a table in the smoking section, which somehow seems promising. However, her lips and fingernails are painted black, and you are not certain whether that is promising or not. With your Bic you light her cigarette – which for some reason she calls a *zigaretten*, then light your own cigarillo and offer her a drink. She asks for Jolly Cola, and you think, Oh Jesus Christ, another woman who doesn't drink. Are you an alcoholic? you wonder. But what is love without wine? Who says there's going to be any love anyway? Perhaps there will be some preliminary stuff. A little bit of necking at this smokey corner table might be nice. Even a tad of petting. You wonder what black lipstick is made of, whether it will turn your own lips black.

Even if she only drinks Jolly Cola, you think she must be on something or other. She is rather hectic. Then you remember that in the café when you first met her, she was somewhat hectic, too, but you didn't really notice that then because you were looking at her breasts. You old pig, you think. Now, however, even her breasts and black lips cannot distract you from her hectic manner. She is flailing about with her hands and arms and talking a mile a minute, mostly about musicians you've never heard or even heard *of.*

Have you ever listened to any music at all? she snaps. I mean in this century! You've got to keep up if you don't want to get old! she says and begins telling about another new indie band.

You try to interject a few words, tell her one of your selected anecdotes, but she interrupts before you are finished. You wonder if you are now a garrulous, boring old dude. You try telling a succinct, tried-and-true, ironic story which invariably gets a laugh, but she takes it literally, totally missing the point. She seems to want only to talk herself.

So, you ask, how have you been?

Terrible! she says. I broke up with my GF and my cat died!

That's terrible, you agree. What's a GF?

She gives you a look. Girlfriend, she says.

That's terrible, you say again,. How did the cat die? *Did she say girlfriend?*

Old age, she says wth a shrug of acquiescence to the inevitability of death when a creature is very old. The cat was, in fact, nineteen years old she tells you – which, you calculate, must be, like, ninety-six in human years.

Are you an animal person? she asks.

You almost wink and say, *Just an animal*, but check yourself in time. Not really, you say instead, realizing how hopeless this is.

You're allergic to cats, and she did say girlfriend, and she doesn't drink. You are not a homophobe but it seems the only thing the two of you have in common is that you both like pussy. And you are not an alcoholic, you assure yourself, but you do like your beer which, as an Irish woman once told you, is a good man's weakness. After another hectic hour, she tells you that she really has to start "circulating."

You say, I was just leaving anyway.

She leaps up and throws her arms around you. It is nice to have your arms around her for a moment. Her slender back is warm beneath your palms. Maybe she also likes men, you think, but what's the point? You don your beret and thank her for a lovely evening and are out the door just as the first group starts up, and you think how fucked all these silly meetings are.

Why, you wonder, did she invite you out when she already said she knew you weren't gay. The question answers itself. She thought you were up above the tree-line, where sex is irrelevant. A clean old male companion.

You don't need this, you think. You can make it on your own. You can be alone. But you remember the very old, very overweight woman you saw on the street this afternoon, leaning across the handlebars of a bicycle she pushed along the street, clearly the only way she was able to keep upright and walk to the supermarket to shop, and you felt a heartrending sadness on her behalf which was, in fact, self-pity. You were picturing yourself unattractive and very old and alone and at the mercy of your loneliness.

The buses are still not running. You flag a taxi and get home and sit on your sofa, still wearing your overcoat and beret, sipping a vodka. Then you check your email. A woman poet you know in the states has sent a message which she signs "Kissiefooples."

You think it is a silly word, but are grateful that there is someone in the world who will send you kissiefooples in the middle of the night even if she is happily married and only flirting harmlessly. You send her kissiefooples back. She answers immediately, saying that only a real man would return kissiefooples and gives you a few more.

In the living room with one last nightcap, you drag out your boxed Motown Collection and put on the Miracles doing "OOO Baby Baby," released on March 5th, 1965, when you were a mere lad of twenty years with a summer girlfriend named JoAnn who had a sweet underslung smile and blue Italian eyes with which she used to watch excitedly how her breasts excited you when you unbuttoned her blouse, and brought you once, out of the kindness of her heart a big bag of pistachios for no reason other than that you had mentioned you liked them, you used to kiss and hug and rub together under the Rockaway Beach boardwalk at 108th Street, and now forty-three years later, you cradle your Irish crystal rock glass against your heart, cubes clinking rhythmically as you step and turn across the plank floor to the smooth intonations of Smokey Robinson singing about needing love, mistakes, mine, yours, about being only human, about crying, dying, leading up to the refrain that is a sweetly melodic moan of romantic yearning, "OOO Baby Baby," and you are dancing with JoAnn of the sweet underslung smile, you are dancing with Bodil again, back then, before, when you were the love of each other's lives, you are dancing with the cute colleague you almost but never, and with all the girls you have ever admired, liked, loved, kissed, longed for and lost but still have now anyway because nothing is ever really lost, not moments of love, they stay with you, and you are dancing now with the very embodiment of woman to whom your complimentary body, your complimentary soul cries out across these small hours of city night, your eyes closed, head tipped back, a smile of yearning ecstasy upon your lips as though you still have a leftover life to live, a babybaby love to hold so close in your dancing embrace, through the romance of yet another summer with its sweet nights of leaf-stirring grass-rippling breezes back when rock and roll was young and pure – "OOO baby baby…I'm dyin'…" as your feet step across the wood plank floor in your little darkened living room, snow falling on the dark courtyard out back – *See, baby?* you whisper to your vodka. *See the snow?* – as your leather shoes keep stepping, you could have been Gene Kelly the way he smiled and closed his eyes dancing with the pleasure of having met a girl he fell for, throughout the two minutes and forty-two seconds until the laser stops tracking, the song ends, the Miracles fall still, gone, until nothing remains save the silence of the deep night, the silently falling snow, and you chuckle at your own folly and down the remainder of your drink.

Goodnight, you whisper. And thanks for all the kissiefooples.

Things could not really be so hopeless, you think. You remember that not two years ago a very attractive physiotherapist of your acquaintance looked frankly into your eyes and said, without the least provocation, I like you. Very much. Then smiled naughtily and added, But you're married! And giggled with her tongue stuck between her teeth. You begin to rummage through your things for her telephone number, but remember then that in the meantime she herself has married. Still, it is evidence of having recently been desired.

Perhaps, you think, you need help.

You phone a psychologist friend and suggest lunch, meet him in a café near his office. He asks how you're holding up, and you say that you think you are ready to meet someone new. He tells you to remember not to sell yourself short, to remember that your market value is high, that you are a good catch. He asks if you noticed the young pretty waitress smiling at you. You tell him that's her job, and he laughs, says, Just a reality check. He advises you to remember that you do not have to agree to anything you do not wish to, to be a warrior and to allow your masculinity to come forth, not to allow a situation in which a power vacuum arises because women tend to try to fill such a vacuum with their own premises.

He looks off in the distance for a moment and says wonderingly, I wonder why they do that?

With a felt-tip pen he jots a list of words on a paper napkin. Beneath the underlined heading "Love," he enumerates points: 1) Checks and balances. 2) The power struggle about the premises. 3) Who you choose. He hands you the napkin which you fold and tuck into your shirt pocket. You feel charged, empowered. You thank him warmly, shake his hand. On the corner he embraces you, lifts one cautionary finger, says, *Remember!*

You pat your coat over the breast pocket in which the napkin is folded, say, I will! I will remember.

At home, you remove and unfold the napkin, read the words jotted there. Premises? you wonder. Checks and balances?

———————

Nonetheless, you try again.

Friday evening, you comb your thinning hair, which you must confess is no longer completely brown. Is, in fact, quite completely grey. But at least you *have* hair, even if hair is no longer very fashionable. You slap an aromatic bracer onto your undeniably veiny cheeks, scrutinize your kisser in the mirror: Will a woman ever love that dew-lapped face again? You brush the shoulders of your navy blue overcoat, slip it on, wrap a long wool scarf about your throat, don your Parisian beret which the ladies seem to like and step out onto the icy Copenhagen street. You overheard a young customer of the woman who trims your hair recommending a place on the north side called the Blue Yard Drugstore. She said, *The northside has such a bad reputation, but this place is soooo cozy. They have music; people even dance! All kinds of people!*

Notwithstanding your romantic solitary cutting of the rug the other night, you sincerely hope you will not be called upon to dance.

Walking briskly to warm your blood, you time yourself. Not quite half an hour from door to door. No bus for this old duffer even if they *are* running again. Get your cardiovasculars pumping, man! Earn your beer.

The Blue Yard Drugstore is an old pharmacy converted to a serving house. It is on Blue Yard Square, lots of clear windows, inviting, a nice place in a shabby area. Sign of incipient gentrification perhaps, although you read in the newspaper that two people were gunned down here recently in an apparent drug-related conflict. You picture yourself doing a Jimmie Cagney death scene. Or just winged. A late-middle-aged nurse bandaging your shoulder, enquiring with admiration about your adventure.

You step in, turn your back on the clientele to blow your nose, then smile and move up to the bar, surveying quickly the age range seated at the tables. Youngish to younger. The bartender is friendly and quick and soon you are seated alone at a smoking-section table for four with a pint of Carlsberg. You continue to favor Carlsberg beer and Hirschsprung small cigars because they support the arts.

You think about the fact that you left New York for Ireland, left Ireland for Denmark half your lifetime ago. Did it for a woman. You think of Fergus, the old bard: *We followed the rump of a misguiding woman. Happy the chair beneath her. I see a land where I could bury my weapon.* With the years your passion calmed which seemed to you natural, cozy, until the coziness stagnated, and you both began to look outward, and you found Bodil, the love of your life, and you the love of hers, until she jerked the rug beneath your feet. Took up with Alphonse, the analyst, is now what you are increasingly certain she did – analyst, your ass, an autodidact, a bank clerk who took a correspondence course, specializing in women. How could you have been so blind? A

67-year-old dandy named Alphonse, he took to hanging about your and Bodil's place, listening with cocked ear whenever you spoke.

"So," said Alphonse, "I hear you saying…" And, "Tell me, how does that make you feel?" When Bodil suggested that you move out of the bedroom and into the spare room down the hall, you said to her, "I hear you saying you want me out of your bed. That makes me feel bad."

Alphonse, listening from the kitchen where he was brewing a pot of chamomile tea – what kind of man drinks chamomile tea?! – called out, "Sarcasm generally masks feelings of insufficiency!"

So, instead of moving down the hall, you moved into a new apartment to start a new life, another new life. Had the old one ever really started? Perhaps. And in its beginning was its end.

You never learn, you think. You're too nice. Women prefer bullies. Can't stand a power vacuum. They try to fill it up with all their premises, and if you let them, they lose respect, order you to move down the hall, make room in their bed for the autodidact dandy. How does that make you feel? Like *shit*, Alphonse. Like shit.

You consider yourself a man of understanding. To understand is to forgive. You forgive everybody everything – everybody except yourself. For you know how despicably unforgiveable you are. I hear you saying you don't forgive yourself. How does that make you feel? Unforgiven.

You sip your pint – not really a pint, four tenths of a liter, not counting the foam, which you wipe from your lips with the back of your ageing freckled hand before looking about. The place is filling rapidly, as a technician sets up sound equipment on the little stage area. An acoustic guitar and a microphone. Not promising. The musician, a tall slender young man, sits on a tall stool and begins to sing a song whose refrain is *Love me love me love me/Love me good…* You do not like the song. You do not like the young man's voice. Nor do you like the young man's face. The young women in the café are flocking about the stage, crying *Vilhelm! Vilhelm*! Which seems to you unfair, that he has that advantage the minstrel classically has in literature and life. To you, he looks rather like a younger version of Alphonse – same pampered little Vandyke around red fleshy lips. You do not want to hear the man singing. The faces at the tables are all young and clean-scrubbed, a few with blond or chestnut beards, girls with the look of a fresh-minted coin, not yet smudged by handling. You finger your dewlaps, note two young couples gazing hungrily at your table, drink up and stand, nod to them and they swarm in with greedy joy and false gratitude.

On with the greatcoat, rewrap the scarf about the throat, beret atop the skull and take it on the arches once again, out into the night seeking a warm place where a woman might serve you food. And a few doors down on Blue Yard Street, you stumble upon Kate's Joint . You dine on lamb curry and two pints of Hof amidst the primitive faces of paintings which watch you, questioning: How does this make you feel? The waitress, a striking young woman with skin the color of café au lait, smiles and says she enjoyed hearing you read your poetry translations at the Poetic Bureau a few weeks ago.

You say, That makes me feel good.

And it does. Goes straight to the refurbishment of the feel-good shield you have been saving from your human-potentialist days and protects you out in the freezing dark night again as the thin soles of your leather shoes lead you deeper north, through the dark of side streets where a skinny leopard-spotted cat watches you from the mouth of a dark alley. You are lost. Far past the mid-point of your life.

A wandering band of boys in hooded jackets begins to chuck empty bottles like hand grenades which explode around you against brick walls in a rain of glass. You make yourself invisible as you continue deeper north. *Past Eve and Adam's by a commodious vicus of recirculation*, etc., you enter the first place that presents itself: through the banged-up face of a serving house whose name you do not note on a street whose name you will not later recall.

Here, despite the world's general declaration of all smokers as miscreants to be freely kicked and insulted, you are allowed to smoke your little cigars, thus supporting the arts, and enjoy bottled Carlsberg Hof at a modest tariff. Straight from the bottle since the glass provided is not something you want near your lips. Surreptitiously you make a quick inventory of your fellow patrons at the other tables and along the bar, glimpse a broken nose, vacant ageing female eyes of blue, hunched shoulders, scuffed and dirty shoes. But the beer is icy cold, as you like it, and you offer compliments to the barmaid, whose dour bulldog puss cracks into a grin as she serves you another. Was that grin flirtatious? That is not what you meant at all.

From your table against the wall, you can see around the elbow of the bar a slender woman in a blue beret cocked jauntily across her head, perched on a stool, eyes closed beatifically above her smiling mouth, dancing ethereally with her hands and arms to Eva Cassidy's "Autumn Leaves" which seeps moodily from the juke box.

The music ends, and the woman in the blue beret opens her eyes and looks directly into yours. She smiles. You avert your gaze, think of Patrick Kavanagh's *Great Hunger: He was suspicious as a rat at the smell of strange bread if a woman smiled at him.* You turn your face to her again and smile, nod.

The juke box is just beside you; she drifts across the floor to study the selections, speaking softly to the machine in Norwegian-accented Danish:

I am old, she tells the juke. I must find old music.

You're by no means old! you exclaim in Irish-American accented Danish. And she is not. Just under two decades your junior – or junioress. An acceptable difference, is it not?

She beams at you, and you observe her face. The features

have been handled a bit by time as you like features to be.

Is my music okay? she asks.

Your music is perfect, you say.

Her dancing hand snakes toward yours and rewards it with a warm clasp. *Soft hand. O touch me! Give us a touch, I'm dying for it.*

I am Norwegian, she says.

I thought you might be, you say, wondering what precisely to do now.

You thought I might be, she repeats, eyes sparkling, as though you have said something truly witty.

She selects Santana and Leonard Cohen and stands a little away from your table, dancing in a trance-like state which does not preclude sly glances toward where you sit, presumably (you fancy) to see if you are watching. And how could you not be?

Do you mind that I dance here all alone? she asks.

You are a pleasure to watch, you reply, wondering if you dare to stand and move your creaky body alongside her slender willowy one. Bodil was the only woman you have ever been able to dance with, who could follow the erratic movements of your ir-rhythms. And what might it entail to try to dance here now with this stranger? Might she have a boyfriend among this battered crowd? Someone who might take exception to your attentions? Or a pimp even? Demanding money? What might be wrong with her that she smiled at you?

She is indeed a pleasure to watch. She has a kind of shawl wrapped smartly about her hips, tied at the waist to fall apart in front, and she moves with grace, turning to allow you (you fancy) a view from all alluring angles, throwing in the occasional discreet bump and grind, and your mind shifts into analytical mode, producing the thought, *She is really quite pickled.* At least twice as more so than you are.

At just that moment a tall, broad-shouldered man with large hands and a baby face approaches your table and plops down into an empty chair, saying, "Mind if I...?" Tattoos show on every exposed area of his skin. On the thick fingers of either hand are tattooed letters spelling out, on the right, R O C K, and on the left, R O L L. Elaborate tattoos crawl out of his shirt collar to wrap about his neck and up around his shaved skull; from the flat of his inner wrist, Elvis Presley's cocked lips sneer.

So, you think. Now the business proposition, the price.

The boy lights a nonfiltered Cecil and says to you, "I'm a young rock and roller. And I think you are an old rock and roller." Enough of a speech to display a hefty slur. Not a pimp, just another drunk. "I got these words tattooed on my fingers when my father died. I was fifteen. He was an old rock and roller, too. So I'm second generation rock and roller."

Moved, you think to share with him a story from your own 15th year, the dawn of R&R, when you were still in New York, about the day in 1959 when you were taking the GG subway home to Queens from your high school in Brooklyn, and the door between the subway cars slid open; in stepped a tall black man of perhaps forty years – an old cat, but cool. His white shirt was unbuttoned, shirt tails untucked, revealing the black skin of his chest, and he was carrying a white handkerchief, flapped out and dangling from his one hand.

In a melodious growl, he announced to the subway car - which was full of boys and girls on their way home from two adjacent Catholic high schools, one for each sex -- "Ever' body on this train: Do rock an' roll!"

And he began to dance along the aisle to the rhythm of the train's shuttling, screeching wheels against the tracks, the rhythms of the cars racketing against one another, dancing to the music his body made from all those sounds, and pointing to each boy or girl as he passed, directing, "You there, boy: Do rock an' roll! And you there, girl: Do rock and roll!" Dancing, twisting, leaping, landing lightly on the toes of his black leather wingtips until he had traversed the length of the car and disappeared out the door at the far end, leaving all the Catholic boys and girls smiling shyly at one another and wishing, just wishing that they might have risen to rock and roll like that man, just one little piece of his infectious, hypnotic set of moves.

That was in 1959 -- 50 years ago. And you wish to impart that tale to this young Danish rock and roller in this wild north side Copenhagen bar where the short, squat barmaid looks like she might once have been a pugilist, and the lovely pickled Norwegian woman sways ethereally to Leonard Cohen's "I'm Your Man," treating you to shy, sly glances from her shining eyes, as you labor in your accented, though functional Danish to tell your tale, to which the drunken young Danish rock and roller's response is, "How long you been living in Denmark? You got a fucking terrible accent! How come you won't learn to speak Danish right?!"

You shrug, smile, fold shut the petals of your story and shove it deep back into your pocket, feeling sad for this young fatherless guy who, despite all the advantages of youth, is so clearly lost.

While telling your tale and partaking of further bottles of Carlsberg Hof, thus supporting the arts, you are vaguely aware of last call being called, of the Norwegian woman with the blue beret leaning close beside you for a moment to murmur at your ear, "Last call, last music, last dance," of people filing out, her blue beret disappearing with one last glance back through the door.

The juke box plays a new song now, Neil Young, "Old Man," and you wonder just how old the Norwegian woman actually was, how much younger than yourself, and just how tipsy she might actually have been, how tipsy you yourself are by now.

With some sense of urgency, you excuse yourself from the young man, take your coat from the hook on the wall, and shrugging it on, long wool scarf trailing behind, you hasten out into the icy dark street. You look right. You look left. The street is empty. The night is old. You button your coat and fling the scarf around your throat, begin your slow walk to find a bus stop.

From somewhere behind an invisible window in a dark wall of apartments up above, you hear the cry of a baby. It makes you feel sad.

———————

Friday, as usual, is followed by Saturday, a new day. You try the opposite end of town, what used to be called The Piss Border. You enter Café Floss, crowded with colorful people. You spot an empty seat at a table where a young man is lapping the Carlsberg from his pint glass with a tongue that is forked; he notices you watching and explains that it has been surgically altered to that state for certain piquant purposes. You notice another empty chair at the next table and move over; you find yourself alongside a young woman with an angelic face and begin to tell her about the fellow with the forked tongue. She invites you to touch the holes where a multitude of piercings have recently been removed from her face; she tells you she is twenty-seven now and no longer feels the need to be pierced. The contact of your fingertips against the holes in her face has aroused tenderness in you. Against your better judgement you ask whether she has ever considered the advantages of love with an older man, and she tells you she does not judge a man by his age but by his aura and that your aura appears to check out.

Then she asks, "How old *are* you?"

You tell her that you were born fifteen years before Denmark entered the European Economic Community. She considers that. Then she roots into her bag for a pen and jots her name, Diete, and telephone number on the back of a soggy coaster. She hugs you and tells you to give her a call.

At home you stick the coaster on a magnet to your refrigerator door where it dries and warps and the lettering and numbers blur. You can still read them, but every time you do the honest math, 64 minus 27 still equals an ancient fool.

An early birthday card arrives from an old girlfriend who lives thousands of miles away. You haven't seen her in decades. You are touched that she continues to remember your birthday. Printed on the front of the card are the Hallmark words "Because you're special..." and she has underlined the word "special" three times. Inside she has written, "I send hugs and kisses from my heart to yours." You read the message several times, feel inordinately cheered. Then you read it once more and wonder if she meant these hugs and kisses to be non-physical ones – from heart to heart but not body to body.

You stand the card on the end table in your living room and gaze at it. You want your kisses not from heart to heart. You want them on your mouth. You want hungry, passionate kisses, bodies and mouths cleaving together, complete with plunging tongues. Then, for some reason, you remember a woman a couple of years back at a reception who was coming on to you with such excess that you excused yourself abruptly and offended her. "You are *pathetic!*" she flung after you. Which you realize that you remembered at just this moment because you *are* pathetic.

What is wrong with you?

What you need to do, you decide, is to immerse yourself in work, bring yourself up to date. Forget hanky-panky. Sublimate. Hanky-panky will come when it comes. If it comes.

You rise early next day and begin to finish reading Junot Dìaz's *The Brief Wondrous Life of Oscar Wao*. You see a similarity between Oscar and you. While you're reading, the postman comes with the latest copy of *the New Yorker*, which you receive two weeks later than everyone in the U.S. You tear off the protective wrapping and begin leafing through, pause to begin reading an article about Donald Barthelme. Then you receive an email from your editor, informing you that the novel you have written which seems to you the best work you have ever done is going to be published in March, and you go to the bookcase shelf on which you have stacked all your own books and manuscripts and slide it out and begin to read. Then you notice that the Saturday book supplement splashed across the table has a review of Dìaz's novel in Danish. You send him an email offering to translate the review for him and he writes back immediately that that would be great but he is sure you have better things to do. You mail him back that you are, in fact, immersing yourself in work for reasons of spirituality and drag out your thick red Danish-English dictionary and begin to translate the review which helps you stop thinking of the Norwegian woman with the blue beret and heart-to-heart kisses and the very soft perforated skin of the 27-year-old Diete's face and all the hanky-panky that might have been.

Time passes in the sweet immersion of linguistic labor. But something goes wrong.

You go and get your beard trapped in the mailbox. The thing is, do you tell everyone and turn it into a big joke on yourself? Or do you keep it a secret? Something of loss-cutting in either approach.

Then you notice that your hands are trembling, which frightens you. Your daughter, a few days ago, in response to something or other you said or did or forgot to say or do, muttered, "Alzheimer's." Then, "Just kidding." It was that *just kidding* that scared you.

But yes – in your defense – "In my defense," you think – you were multi-tasking quite drastically. By turns you were reading the Díaz novel, translating the review from Danish, reading that *New Yorker* review of the new biography of Barthelme, much of whose work you admire, some of which you do not get and/or appreciate and at least one of which (*Snow White*) you find fatuous (you take a moment from your other tasks to check your Webster's to be certain 'fatuous' really means what you think it means – it does), were rereading the manuscript of your own new novel which is about to be published by an "important" house; you have important doubts it will be greeted as important, though rereading it, you are at one and the same time impressed with the writing but also unable quite to remember ever having written it. That was only three years ago. You wonder if you could still write something like that. Can a mind deteriorate in just three years? *Your* mind?

In the midst of juggling these tasks, this hornet's nest of thoughts, you are at least pleased to note that it is 4:00 p.m. and you have not had a drink all day, while the review you are reading of the Barthelme biography notes that *he* usually had *his* first drink of the day at noon (so, sometimes, do you, although far from usually and not today and you are 64 while B died at 58, as did your own father) and then you remember you have no wine to drink with your entrecote this evening and, in fact, no entrecote either, or fat to fry it in, and you admonish yourself (check the Webster's again – yes, *admonish yourself*) to nip out to the supermarket before it closes to purchase those items (wine, steak, fat).

And you do that.

Pleased to find that it is snowing, that the snow is sticking to the cobblestones, parked cars, window ledges, pavement, bare black bones of the trees. Snow is so cheery. You are cheered.

However, in the course of tallying up your wares, the Calibanesque cash-register teenager – who fairly slams your steaks (you bought two even though you live alone – never know if you'll get lucky, even if your last piece of luck was back around a no-longer visible corner of time) onto the conveyer belt and without so much as a glance your way slaps your change onto the change dish which rouses your fury (*Pimply godamned creep!* you think), followed immediately by remorse for even in your thoughts so despising another human being who no doubt suffers for the boils on his face and slouch of his posture.

Then, congratulating yourself for having remembered all the items you went out for, on the way home along the snowy February sidewalk, snow still falling cheerily, the chill seeping up through your thin leather soles, you review your thoughts in search of one you feel you ought to remember and do remember again, that you are now six years older than either Barthelme or your own father when they died (and considering the fact that B's father apparently had been less kind than had yours who, for all his failings, at least never poked a thumb into your cupcakes or snapped in half your unbreakable LPs to prove that they were in fact not unbreakable, which the article in *the New Yorker* reported that B's father had done). Then you also remember that in three weeks you will be sixty-five and have not yet decided whether to have a party for that occasion, though you have in some way to commemorate the event for you have more or less promised your son and daughter that you will do so, then remember your plan of inviting the two of them on an overnight cruise to Oslo where you will show them the incredible Tomba Emanuel, with its striking juxtaposition of images of sex and death, which you are certain will amaze them, make them think good old dad has a trick or two up his old sleeve, and still have time for lunch at the Grand Café (where Ibsen used to dine) and catch the boat back to Copenhagen.

Vacantly, you stand for a moment on the white creaking planks of your kitchen floor amidst the white walls and cabinets, staring out the slightly-opened white-framed window to the snow-white courtyard and recall an image from the Tomba Emanuel painted vividly on the black wall by Gustav Vigeland's little brother just about the same year you yourself were born: Voluptuous naked body of a long-limbed, large-breasted woman giving birth to a bleached-white death's head. Your body shivers with the remembered image, and you look around you, recalling the present moment, what you were doing, and pick your wares out of the bag to place them in the refrigerator, step out to the living room, but then return to the kitchen and remove the bottle of Cabernet from the ice box with a muttering shake of your head.

Something, you think then, has been calling for action. You finger back through your thoughts to try to recall – wine in the ice box, woman on black wall, bleached-white skull between her thighs, Tomba Emanuel and – *Oslo!*

Now you stand over the kidney-shaped coffee table upon which lies the Dìaz book and *the New Yorker* folded open to the Barthelme article, thinking you have at least completed the translation of the Dìaz review, but before anything else, you sit down to your computer and key in DFDS Seaways, click on "Order journey," click on "Country: Norway," and arrange electronically for the three of you, father-daughter-son, to sail to Oslo and back for your 65th birthday, sleeping in an outside cabin for three, with porthole view of the billowing cold green sea, order a three-course meal on the way up and a three-course gourmet meal on the way back because that will be your birthday, all for $900, not bad at all, quickly recheck each item of the order, fill in your credit card details, muttering curses as you squint at the glossy hard-to-read numerals on the face of the card and the new fangled three-digit code on the obverse, and click "Confirm," receive your confirmation number and itinerary only to find that in fact what you have irrevocably ordered is not a cruise Copehagen-Oslo-Copenhagen, but Oslo-Copenhagen-Oslo, and since it is now Saturday, you cannot speak to a human being in the DFDS Seaways offices: *You have three choices, press one if your call...* etc., and you press the appropriate number to learn the offices are closed until Monday morning, whereupon your mouth opens to emit from deep in your lungs a shout of "SHIT! Shit shit SHIT!" Then you remember that the kitchen window is open, so lower your voice and mutter a quiet, "Shit," already doubting, however, that any amount of arguing, flattery or begging will result in a reversal of your irrevocable order.

That is when your hands began to tremble.

Not because of the money so much as because you have made this mistake, this old man's failing-witted mistake.

Worse case scenario, you reason then: Monday morning 8:00 a.m., you phone Oslo and get on the phone a true-blue square-head who says, Sorry, sir. You clicked that you agree to the terms and conditions where it is clearly stated that the sale is irrevocable once you click confirm, and you did click confirm. Sir.

Is none of it refundable? Must I pay for the dinners that we will not even be there to eat?

Sorry, sir.

Okay okay okay, you tell yourself. Worst-case scenario: you lose $900. You will reorder the journey in reverse. You will do so not electronically but speaking with a human being who will guide you through the process, even if it winds up that you have to pay for the correct journey as well as the incorrect journey. So it will cost you double what it should have cost. You will make other economies to balance that, and you will never mention it to anyone. You will chalk it up to proverbial experience. No one need ever know.

But *you* will know.

And that is when, with trembling hands, you pour your first drink of the day. At 5:55 p.m. A hefty vodka on the rocks. And halfway through the drink, you do feel better.

You've just got to slow down, you think and take another sip, noticing that you are more than halfway through your hefty drink. You are, in fact, already down to the place where the ice cubes, not even melted even a little bit yet, click against your teeth, and you can refill the glass without even replenishing the ice. Which – after striking your forehead three painful blows with your fist (well, somewhat painful – uncomfortable at least) – you do.

Now it is 6:14 p.m. on the Saturday of a weekend you cleared of all social obligations – as if you had so many! – in order to catch up on things. So you are alone with a multitude of half-done multitasks – well some of them are done, but one done incorrectly at the cost of nine hundred goddamn wasted dollars – and no one is around to share your tale of woe, more specifically no woman to draw your throbbing forehead (you really hurt your head!) against her breasts and smooth your thinning hair gently, saying, "There there. There there. You poor guy you. Could happen to anybody."

And why should she comfort you anyway? She needs her own comfort for her own woes. And you realize with that thought that you were thinking of poor Bodil, the memory of whom could make you weep, even though she kicked you out in favor of her irritating Vandyke-bearded autodidact analyst Alphonse, or maybe that is just something you are thinking to excuse yourself, maybe she just kicked you out because you are not good enough, or because she did not really love you, or no longer loved you, no longer needed your ancient worthless love, making you doubt that the love she had lavished upon you all those years had ever really been any more than self-deception on her part, the wish to love, to objectify you as her beloved just as you had (perhaps) objectified her body, her mouth, her smile, her eyes, her delicate sculpted hands with red-painted nails, her gentle manner as the embodiment of Woman but you know on some level that things have gone awry in her pretty little head way back when she started seeing the analyst (analyst, your ass! A bank clerk with a correspondence course diploma!) and writing all those angry letters to all those who had displeased her, and everyone except the autodidact analyst had displeased her – her priest, the mayor, her publisher, her editor, gallery owner, daughters, sister… They all got long letters, single-spaced, several-paged arrangements of the facts according to Bodil, and finally of course, you got one, too, explaining that she would be gone for a fortnight at the end of which she expected you to be gone forever unless you would fulfill certain conditions (move into the spare room, remove all your things from the bedroom which would now be hers to dispose of as she pleased and off limits except and unless she invited you in, confine your activities to the spare room, separate from hers your books, CDs, DVDs, and – this, she assured you, was the foundation of any future you might have together – democratize your economies, which seemed to mean that she wanted to stick a drinking straw into your capital.)

So instead of moving into the spare room, you moved into a completely new apartment and left her alone with her failing wits to find now that your own wits are failing as well.

And she continues to send you and your children, too, and some of your friends, strange vaguely poisonous single-spaced letters detailing remembered grievances, the love of your life who used to tell you that you were, at last, the love of hers, so you can only conclude that love is an illusion, or the kind of love you had come to expect or hope for is an illusion, for everyone in essence is born alone, lives alone, dies alone, with nothing but illusions as comrades, illusions as consolation, and when you dream and when you love, you embrace phantoms for what in this temporal existence is really real? Is real even real?

No, you think then. No. Some communication between human beings can at least be of substance. Can't it?

Just that afternoon you received a mail from a woman you know who had written an excellent article – an excellent communication – which had been rejected by one newspaper, and you urged her to submit it to another, but she wrote back, "It would be no use, they would reject it, too," and you shot back another mail at her saying, "A door won't open if you do not knock. And you cannot win if you do not play." To which she responded, "Ow! You stepped on a sore toe. I don't even know if I really want to play." And you have not yet responded to that.

Do it now! you command yourself.

But still you sit on the sofa surrounded by all your books, pads, tasks, your freshly poured vodka close to hand, nine hundred goddamned stinking dollars poorer for your feeble-brained stupidity, and you think of your father, dead at fifty-eight, and Donald Barthelme also dead at fifty-eight, and Andre Dubus dead at 61 and John Updike recently dead at 76, and you think, I am losing it, I am now losing it, and what awaits you in the not-so-distant future is decerebration and/or death. *You* will be the naked, grinning, bleached-white skull, skull-alone in a dark place between the luscious thighs painted on the black wall.

You gaze out the window at the courtyard. It has stopped snowing. Which seems somehow very sad. And you think you might weep, but actually what you need to do is to micturate. So you get up and walk across the Persian carpet you are so fond of that covers the raw plank floor you are also fond of, and you knock on the bathroom door, then remember that you live alone so no one is in there. You open the door, lift the lid and do just that, micturate.

It is a pleasure, a relief. Something, at your age, to be thankful for. And you are.

You say aloud, "Be thankful for that at least." And, "I *am* thankful."

Following which, you flush, put down the lid, wash your fingers and go back to work.

But instead of working, you stand at the window, gazing out to the white courtyard, the virgin snow not yet trodden by human feet.

In less than three weeks, you think – because come Monday you will correct that error, even if it ends by costing you an extra nine hundred dollars – you will be on the Oslo boat with your now adult children, dining. They will toast your 65th birthday, and in their eyes you will see reflected the old man that you have become.

But then, in the morning, the boat will dock in Oslo, and you will spirit them along the quay to the taxi rank. You will occupy the seat beside the driver and ask him to take you to the Slemdal section and to wait while the three of you go into the strange museum, ducking your heads beneath the low doorway, above which are Emmanuelle Vigeland's ashes in an urn, and the three of you will stand in the high, black, vaulted room, and you will observe the voluptuous thighs painted on the black wall giving birth to the bleached-white skull and hear the eerie whispers of your three intermingled breathings amplified by the room's seeming supernatural acoustics, and then you will go out to the taxi, which will carry the three of you to the Grand Café on Karl Johannes Gate while you tell your son and your daughter about how ahead of his time Ibsen, who used to dine there, was, and how James Joyce's very first publication, at the age of eighteen, was a review of Ibsen's very last play, *When We Dead Awaken*, and you will quote for them the lines –

We only see what we have missed

When we dead awaken.

And what then do we see?

We see that we have never lived. –

and over your lunch plates in the Grand Café, your children will lift their glasses of red wine to toast you once again on your 65th birthday, and you will see reflected in their eyes that the old man, after all, still has a trick or two up his good old sleeve.

YOUR RELATIONSHIP IS GOING THROUGH BAD WEATHER

Trying to walk off dark hours and thoughts of Bodil, thoughts of Carlita Cicerone a former student you have been dreaming about of late, and the shock of suddenly recognizing that you are a sixty-five year old orphan, you find yourself wandering Isted Street, not far from the Central Station, the wild west side of this ancient capital. It is late, the cold sidewalks empty, the black leather and pink and lavender dildos of porn shop windows dimly illuminated. Doubling back toward the station to avoid a group of beefy flaneurs, you pass a doorway from the shadows of which a woman asks, You vant to come op with me?

You have not really considered this sort of alternative to loneliness. You pause to look at her, feel yourself swaying slightly, having stopped here and there for a pint. You doubt that you would be able to muster passion for this woman, whose bare legs in a mini skirt are bone-thin and purple with chill. You look at her face, which vaguely resembles the face of The Little Mermaid, her dirty blond hair short and choppy and her complexion, even shadowed, not the best. You do wish to die the little death at least one more time before you die the big one, but you wish to do so with someone other than this poor creature in the shadows of that doorway, and neither do you wish to purchase that little death, at least not with money.

Nonetheless, the heart in your head goes out to her. Perhaps you would increase the sum of human misery by blatantly rejecting her. The head in your heart suggests that it might by a minuscule measure decrease the sum of human misery if you and this woman, fully clothed and ever so fleetingly, hugged, exchanged momentary warmth in recognition of one another's misery.

How much just for a hug? you ask.

You can't buy no love affair, dude, she says. You want French? Four hundred. Swedish? Three. Danish cost you five plus the room.

You know what French is; Swedish, you guess, is a honeymoon of the hand; while Danish, you presume, is the style of the missionary. Dismal. You shake your head, dig into your pocket for the fifty crown note that is buried there, reach it toward her hand which automatically rises to accept it, and you turn to move on, but she steps out quickly from the shadows, brushes her lips against your cheek. Her blue eyes almost smile. You nod and continue walking. It occurs to you, as you climb the concrete steps from the dark side street up to the Central Station, that you are far out, that it is time to return to your miserable apartment and sleep.

In the morning, sitting on the edge of your bed, you shudder to think of the woman in the shadowy doorway, consider the fact that you could be so far out as to stop on a dark street to consider a poor, wretched hooker. Perhaps you should focus more on the simple, ordinary, everyday things. Cultivate the potential *joie de vivre* in your daily life, the smell of coffee from a newly opened package, the hiss of the broken vacuum, sound of the spoon digging in to the grinds, the plop of mail through the door slot, the newspaper waiting on the mat for you to read, pleasure of the senses, five avenues of communication with existence. Pay attention. Bathe your head in water, dress in clean garments, take brisk walks and observe the world.

You do that, legs pumping you through the streets, past your corner church where, you know, social events are regularly held – art exhibitions, talks, screenings. Parishioners gather over coffee and cake, even a bit of wine, sandwiches. Perhaps you should become a church-goer. You attended briefly with Bodil, who was active there. Until she had a disagreement with the priest, who wanted the congregation to begin kneeling, which she refused to do. Perhaps you should go back. You are not a member, do not pay church tax, but they wouldn't have to know that. You could sit in a back pew in a ray of sunlight during the services, meditate the beatitudes, nothing wrong with the beatitudes, maybe meet a hot widow to practice the little death with. Christians get lonely for a ride, too.

But your legs have left the cozy little church behind, pump you along the boulevard with its pastel apartment buildings. See there, a house where Georg Brandes lived, says it on a plaque, advance guard of the Modern Breakthrough. And slouching toward you a boy, perhaps fourteen, walking with fists stuffed in the slash pockets of his jacket, dressed more for spring than winter, his posture a mix of bravado, shy pleasure and curiosity. You remember yourself at that age, that same mix of expectant emotion. Is that really gone? Yet the heart behind your face is young as his. You order yourself to look at your face, mirrored in a shop window; you refuse the order, suck in your gut and quicken your pace to a brisk clip, smile at the boy, and he smiles back. Excellent lad!

The pounding of your feet sends a sensation to your mouth just as you reach the Coal Square and spy the White Lamb serving house, established 1807, semi-basement across from where Søren

Kierkegaard lived in the 1830s. Wonder did Søren K, in his 20s then, ever nip down as you yourself are now doing for a large draft.

You pick a table near the window, order sardines and a pilsner, help yourself to the morning tabloid provided for the reading pleasure of the patrons. You eat your sardines on rye with knife and fork, press juice from the lemon slice over the two shiny little fish, sip your pilsner, paging through the newspaper, anticipating what awaits you on page 9: *Helga is twenty and comes from Albertslund.* Helga, naked but for some sort of cord around her waist and a very small bird's nest in a very existential place, gazes with raised eyebrows and half-mast lids into the camera. A knowing smile plays across her lips, her body turned three-fourths forward, her small, nonsymmetrical breasts nodding upward. You find it hard to believe that this black and white photograph of a 20-year-old woman, unremarkable in all but the fact that she is naked, can rouse such longing in you.

You wonder if something is wrong with you, whether your humanity is stunted. Should you not be incensed at this objectification of another human being, particularly one so young? Should you not be ashamed to be eyeballing, in order to arouse your lower passions, this young woman, young enough to be your granddaughter – even, by a stretch, your great granddaughter?

You should be ashamed.

But you are not.

Reluctantly, you page on, come to the classified ads toward the back, the many entries under "Massage." You think again about the fact that prostitution is legal in this country, though profiting from it by third parties is not. You remember the skinny woman in the doorway – *Can't buy no love affair, dude!* Well, why not? you think. And the crazy idea fleets through your mind of paying a woman to love you, to pretend to love you, to smile and comfort and lie to you, give you what you like. For one dizzy moment it seems a viable possibility before revealing itself as pathetic madness, then the taint of that madness colors all the love and affection you have ever experienced in your life: Was it all just a sham, a purchase, exchange, barter, I buy a round and then you buy a round, kiss for a kiss, tit for tat, this for that, I take care of you, you take care of me. One long mutual back scratch.

You turn the last page of the massage ads, look at the comics — Beetle Bailey getting pounded by Sarge, Killer's moustache ends twinkling at some foxy WAC, Andy Capp on the sofa raising his head to call for his wife to bring him a beer, Dagwood being bested by Blondie, belted by Bumstead. Turn to Your Stars today: *Your relationship is going through bad weather. Maybe you can't stop the rain but you can build a shelter of kindness and consideration and invite your mate in to get warm.*

Sitting at the table, you gaze out to the chill winter square, remembering things you did wrong with Bodil: Got drunk, acted like a prick, snapped at her. But never called her names. Never. Never hit or pushed or laid angry hands on her. Never. Gave her presents. Loved to love her, to kiss and hug her. Never tired of that. Reach around behind her and cup those lovely melons in your palms, feel the nipples stiffen. Last couple times you did that, she jerked away. Invited her to the sunny south islands. Listened to her. Not always. Not when she gabbed. Misunderstood sometimes. Impatient. Distant.

Did you build a shelter of kindness and consideration and invite her in to get warm? Sometimes. A lot of times!

Then, as your agitation builds, you suddenly see yourself at the age of sixty-fucking-five sitting in this 200-year-old serving house, delivering yourself to agitation from a tabloid horoscope. Abruptly you shove your empty sardine plate from you, quaff the remainder of your pilsner, pull on your long dark overcoat, beret, wrap your long grey-striped scarf around your throat, clip on shades, climb three steps up to the street, stride briskly across the square to the North Gate. Your feet propel you past Rosenborg

Castle, the Botanical Gardens, across Brandes Square where the head of Brandes in bronze sits on a pedestal in thin winter sunlight. Thinking modernist thoughts. Breaking through.

You are walking east, toward your miserable little apartment where you do not want to be, hoping that something will deflect you from that undesired goal. You think of the Fiver Wine Room, quarter of an hour's quick-step from here, enough to build up a thirst, think of sitting there among people who know you by sight, enough to nod, make room for you without imposing, put on the jazz CD you request. Your feet decide, change course, aiming for that quiet place of quiet jazz.

On Silver Street, a tall construction worker wearing dirty white overalls and carrying a rattling plastic bag of beer bottles, handsome man of perhaps fifty, looks you up and down, then demonstratively laughs into your face.

What?!

Why did that man laugh at you? Are you so ridiculous now that strangers feel free to laugh at the sight of you? What is the meaning of this? Dolt! you think. I am not nobody! you think. I am not ludicrous! you think. I am not just any ordinary flea on the backside of god! you think, quoting Charles Simic to enlist your erudition and his linguistic skills for support in your distress.

On Stockholm Street, you stop and peer at your reflection in the window of an antique shop, surveying your image for some trace of absurdity: dark beret, long dark overcoat, long grey scarf, clip-on shades, grey sideburns. What is ludicrous about any of these things?

Perhaps, you think, you look anachronistic. Perhaps you look eccentric. You recall a scrap of literary history – when the editor of the controversial 1840s periodical *Corsaren*, a man named Goldschmidt, with the money he had made from the magazine's success, had purchased an extraordinary greatcoat with gold buttons and epaulettes and gold braiding on the breast and walked out proudly on the Copenhagen streets only to be stopped by Kierkegaard, who advised him that he should not go about in such an extravagantly decorated coat but should dress like others. Mortified, Goldschmidt took the coat back to his tailor and had it modified.

In light of that memory, you wonder if your own appearance seems extravagant to others. You recall that Bodil encouraged you to wear hats, to dress with distinction and style as she herself did. You wonder if it was a folie à deux that has now been reduced by subtraction to a folie à un?

You picture yourself reverting to tweed jackets, white shirts, neckties. No! Or wearing jackets with name brands emblazoned on the left breast. No! You won't! Yet the thought of entering the Fiver Wine Room now, the possibility that behind the nods and smiles might hover suppressed laughter is lodged like a splinter beneath the nail of your heart, and you change course once again, head directly home. You try to picture yourself in the eyes of the world, ask yourself sincerely if you might appear out of kilter. It seems that you no longer know what sort of image will be created in the eyes and minds of others by your appearance and behavior. You wonder, as you have wondered before, if that is the thought process of a psychopath, to be concerned more with the way others see your behavior than with its moral and human correctness and balance. Perhaps you are actually some manner of low-grade psychopath. You once phoned your psychologist friend to enquire whether it was possible that you could be a low-grade psychopath. He chuckled and told you that a psychopath never asks himself whether he is a psychopath. You ask, therefore, you are not, he said.

Still.

Nearly home, you stop on your corner at the convenience shop run by a Pakistani immigrant. Bodil uses this shop, too, so you are always poised for an encounter, although you have only run into her once here. She averted her eyes, turned her back, then sent you a letter suggesting that you choose another convenience shop to avoid the unpleasantness of further meetings. You neither replied nor complied.

Now you load milk, eggs, juice, bacon, licorice, a bottle of wine into the shopping basket, and as the Pakistani loads your goods into a transparent blue plastic bag, he glances at you with a smile that seems to you simpering, perhaps even vulturous – are you going mad? you wonder – and he asks whether you and Bodil are still apart.

You nod, think, What is this? Is he trying to collect gossip?

But are you still good friends? he asks. That simpering smile. Do you still think about her?

Taking your bag of goods, you tell him that is a private matter which you do not wish to discuss.

His smile falters. I ask only as a friend, he says, and you think perhaps this is a cultural difference, perhaps you are out of balance, imagining things.

It's okay, you tell him, but I prefer not to discuss it.

Then you are home with your bag of staples. Still wearing your coat and beret you pour a hefty vodka over ice, light a cigar, sit in the dark on your sofa.

You ought to call your children, you think. But it seems you are always calling them. You have promised yourself to give them room, to wait until *they* call you, fear the thought of them dreading the weekly call from Dad. Picture the two of them discussing you, trading Dad stories. You order yourself to pull yourself together, lay your cigar and untouched drink aside , remove your coat and cap and jacket, put your wares away, drop to the Persian carpet and snap off twenty push-ups, reassured that you are still able to do at least that.

Then, supine on the carpet, you notice a scatter of mail beneath the slot on your front door. A royalty check – always comforting. The new issue of *The New Yorker*. You slit open the envelope with the check -- $421. Every bit helps. You tear the wrapping off *The New Yorker*, relight your cigar, sip your vodka, leaf through the magazine, pause to glance at an article about Ludwig Wittgenstein, learn that three of his four brothers committed suicide, two in their early twenties, the third at forty; that another brother, a concert pianist, lost one arm; that there were three sisters and that the husband of one of them committed suicide also, following the example of his father. The family, it seems, was one of the wealthiest in Austria. The article goes on to say that the one-armed brother achieved success as a concert pianist, that practicing on a grand piano in their home once, he jumped up and shouted through the closed door at his brother in the next room to get out of the house because he could feel his skepticism seeping in beneath the door.

You close the magazine, puff your cigar. The smoke gives comfort, but the outburst of the one-armed concert pianist has you thinking of Bodil's claim that you filled too much space in the living room. You remember one of your brothers saying about the other once that there was not room for anyone else in his presence. You wonder if there could be anything to this sort of claim.

That night you dream about a woman you know who works in a bookshop. In the dream she stops you on the stairway and asks, Have I been too demanding? She studies your face with a penetrating gaze, then kisses you once, twice, three times, her lips gentle and soft, wonderful lips. You fall in love with her but lose your balance and strike your back against the banister.

You wake and look at the illuminated dial of your wristwatch: 4:25 a.m. The clock is set for 6:15, but something else has awakened you.

Pain. In your back, your side. Bad pain. Very bad. Appendicitis? You limp out to your computer, google "appendicitis." Right side. This is the left. And escalating. You limp around the apartment, groaning, instructing yourself not to act like a baby, thinking, God has decided to cut you down in your 65th year, like Chaucer's White Knight: Alone, without any company! What does it matter, you wonder, that you loved jazz and poetry when you are dead? What good did it do you? Which somehow seems ironic and vaguely funny, though the pain does not allow you to laugh. There is a basic background of excruciating pain which every so often notches up and remains at the new level.

Pain this great, you think, cannot continue for long. But it continues. Half an hour. Forty-five minutes. An hour. You lean on a chair back, bow forward across the surface of your writing table, kneel on the floor with your butt in the air and your chest on a cushion, lay on your right side, left side. Nothing helps. You are writhing, in constant motion seeking a position of relief but no relief is to be found.

You try to think. What to do? Emergency room? Call the emergency doctor? What's the number? But your brain is taken up by the pain, no room for thought, trying to fathom it. Without success. Abstract from it. Can't. Now it is an hour and fifteen minutes, and the pain is still constant and very bad. On a scale of 1 to 10? This has its own scale which outweighs all normal measures. Here there's only max.

You baby! Pull yourself together! Can't. *Why do I hurt so bad?*

As the pain moves toward an hour and a half's duration you think, Call your kids. Then you think, No, don't call your kids! You go to the phone and dial information, get the number for the emergency doctor and say, Call up, into the mouth piece. There is a queue on the line, and you are told by a recorded voice that you are number fourteen. Which could only mean a good hour before you get through and then no doubt three or four or five hours before the doctor comes. You call the hospital emergency room to ask for an ambulance. The operator tells you to take a taxi out, so you call a cab and are promised one in ten minutes.

You lay down the phone and run for the bathroom and heave. Twice. Red. Blood? You think of your father who at 58 one day threw up blood, lived on in terrible pain for three days, then died. Your heart goes out to him for those three days of pain. Here you are not quite at two hours and almost willing to die to be free of it.

You cancel the taxi and call back to *demand* an ambulance, explain you can't take a taxi because you are throwing up blood. That works. They are there in less than ten minutes. Two young men. The one says to you, Boy, some way to start the day, huh?

They provide you with a barf bag, strap you to a stretcher, and drive you to the trauma center at The State Hospital – the hospital made famous by Lars Van Trier in his TV series *Riget*, later optioned by Stephen King as *The Kingdom*, although King would have trouble matching Van Trier in terms of intelligent eerie dark humor. At this particular moment your own sense of humor is deactivated. You are rewriting Keats' "Ode on a Grecian Urn." All you know on earth is that pain is truth, truth pain. And that all you wish is to be free of that truth at any cost.

An orderly tells you it is probably a kidney stone you are experiencing and hands you a morphine suppository. Can you do this yourself? he asks.

Do what? you ask and barf into your barf bag.

As repulsive as it is to you, the orderly pulls on clear plastic gloves and shoves the thing up your butt. You are lying on the stretcher in your puke-spattered pajamas with a lump of morphine stuck up your kazoo, staring blurrily at the ceiling and thinking about the White Knight's song:

> *What is this life?*
> *What asketh man to have.*
> *Now with his love*
> *Now in the cold grave.*
> *Alone, without any company.*

Well, you're not in the grave yet anyway, you think. Which is possibly a good thing.

Somewhere around four hours later you notice that the pain seems to have subsided to a distant throb. But you don't trust it to be gone. You feel it there, watching, ready to clamp onto you again when you least expect it.

You realize now that you have never truly known pain before, have learned that pain is another dimension. You realize that you have just had a glimpse of what it is like for anyone stuck in that dimension, which made you understand, graphically, the need for empathy. The irony does not escape you that no one understands the need for empathy as well as one who needs it. And something else has been made quite clear to you as well: You do not wish to visit that dimension again anytime soon, like never.

You thank god that there is an efficient hospital system here to help you deal with that pain. But at the same time you are now acutely aware that there is no longer anyone in your life who will share whatever comes your way and will truly care that you are experiencing pain and stand by you in your pain. Perhaps, you think, we are all in this together. But you, you think, are alone now.

The morning proceeds with a lower body scan which indicates that there are no further stones in your kidneys.

If, the scanologist woman notes, what you experienced *was* a stone.

She tells you that you are being sent up to urology for a bladder probe. You very much do not wish to experience a bladder probe, but in the lingering haze of the kazoo morphine, you cannot find the words that will release you from this further indignity.

Then you are naked on a table, a doctor and a nurse standing over you. The doctor tells you that they just need to have a look in your bladder. You tell the doctor that you experienced this once before, about fifteen years ago and that it hurt like holy hell so you would like to have more morphine first. He explains with a superior smile that great progress has been made over the past fifteen years in equipment and technique, that this will take only a few moments and that you may experience some discomfort but no pain. You have heard that expression before and recognize it for the lie it is, but the nurse disables your resistance with a look of pure empathy. You resign yourself to what they must do.

The doctor asks the nurse to pass him "a number fourteen" which he proceeds to insert into your penis. This is not fun. Even less fun when he says, Oh dear, there is a stricture.

Oh, no! you moan. What is a stricture?

That means that you're, er, narrow, he explains.

We are the narrow men, you mutter — a pathetic bid for dignity.

The doctor says to the nurse, Perhaps we should try a number twelve.

No, you croak, make it a number eight! Make it a number six!

They acknowledge your statement with a chuckle, not realizing apparently that you were not joking.

Okay, then, says the doctor, a number ten. And he proceeds with this long insult to that part of your body that has all your life been so private and pleasurable but which the medical world now seems intent on invading and tormenting.

You stare up at the hazy white ceiling and try to find something to distract your mind while they conduct their invasion and torment. You're a writer, you think: Imagine something! Imagine something other than a woman, something other than a woman's lovely legs, other than...

You advise yourself not even to go there. To think of other joys. Picture a Waterford crystal rock glass in your hand, four clear distilled-water rocks in the glass. Picture a bottle of black label Smirnoff. Uncapped. Picture the triple distilled vodka steaming over the rocks, cracking them. Picture the glass lifting to your lips. Picture removing the stirrer from this lovely potion. Yes, picture that. Picture the stirrer being removed slowly, most gingerly, cast away from you…

You open your eyes and see the empathetic middle-aged face of the nurse looking down into yours. You think you love her, even as you realize she could not possibly feel real empathy for all the many patients that people her days. It must be an act.

We're all done, sir, she whispers.

At first you hear it as "done for," which alarms you, but then, Thank you, you whisper back.

Now the doctor's face is there, too, a bland face devoid of empathy. We found nothing, he says. Your bladder would appear to be a healthy one.

Thank you, you whisper. Thank you so much. Would you please call me a taxi? You can tell by his smile that he is tempted to Groucho Marx you, say, *Okay, you're a taxi*, but instead he says, "The receptionist will do that."

And then you are experiencing the surreal moments of sitting in the back seat of a Mercedes taxi cab, wearing pukey pajamas, your dick smarting smartly, as a new lump of morphine pulses in your kazoo, radiating outwards, and the driver drives you east toward your miserable apartment while telling you about what the hospital system did to him the year before.

Sawed open my chest, he says over his shoulder. Peeled back my ribs and replaced a valve in my heart with the valve of a pig. God's truth! Pig Heart, the wife calls me now. And know what I am? A Jew!

Be thankful, you murmur, uncertain whether you really said it and to whom you are speaking.

In your pocket are three additional morphine suppositories in a plastic envelope which you have been advised to refrigerate as soon as you get home. Home, you think, and picture your tiny apartment with a stack of unwashed dishes in the sink and no woman in your bed. Not that you would be in any condition to respond to her presence, but you would powerfully much like to put your arm around her and hold her face to your chest and inhale the sweet aroma of her hair.

Then you are in your apartment. It is well past noon. You think of frying two eggs, but make toast instead with a slice of cheese and ketchup, remember your mother used to call this a pizza. You were not kind enough to your mother, you think. You drink a tumbler of tomato juice straight down, smack your lips. Your dick hurts. A lot. You place the morphine suppositories in the refrigerator, in the empty butter compartment. You consider inserting a fresh one where it will do you good, but decide instead to load a bong of skunk, locate the little cellophane bag in the cigar box where you keep your postage stamps and airmail stickers and stash, light the bong with a stick match and suck sweet 'moke deep into your lungs, lean back, smiling, and feel the skunk tingle across the soles of your feet, up into your poor tortured clockwork…

Alive!

You have lived to smoke another bong.

Munching the remainder of your cheese on toast, you hobble out to the computer, fire it up, check your Gmail and see through half-lidded eyes a message from Carlita Cicerone, a woman who a few years ago was your student, a blue-eyed Sicilian poet you once kissed. She is now affiliated with an academic conference held in New York during the summer. Attached is a formal letter of invitation for you to speak there, to which Carlita has affixed a ps:

I so hope you can come. It would be lovely to see you again. I've missed you.

It has been a long, long weekend, you think. But Carlita has missed you, might very well, in fact, have been missing you for months, years; even in your greatest distress she might have been missing you, even as the orderly inserted the morphine plug up your butt, she might have been mssing you.

You select the reply tab on your Gmail and, your heart is beating like mad, and you key in *Yes I will...*

LAST NIGHT MY BED A BOAT OF WHISKEY GOING DOWN

The women here are so damn beautiful you are in near constant danger of saying something likely to exact a snapped retort like *Old dudes should not hit on young chicks*, but it is a collision course, and at four p.m. you are already nipping down to the official conference bar. In truth you had already nipped over at lunchtime but that was for a purely reparatory beverage whose purpose was only to winch you back up to par after last night when your bed was a boat of whiskey going down, as Steve Davenport so aptly put it, and your bed no doubt will again be that tonight since you have undoubtedly just traversed the on-ramp to 12-step-city, but you have miles to go yet before Canada runs dry. Good evening, my name is none of your business, and I wish to remain as long as possible just where I am, in blithe denial.

So you had a single Stoli on the rocks, no fruit please, just to soothe your troubled mind and prepare for the series of meetings from two to four, and undeniably the meetings – also with beautiful women, each of whom has paid for thirty minutes of creative advice – went well, and this evening is the official conference banquet and dance but you are already now, after changing your shirt, slipping back under par so you steer back down to the official conference bar, this time for a *double* Stoli on rocks, no fruit please.

On the enormous flat-screen spanning the above-bottle strip of wall like a celestial observation post a beautiful woman is embracing a man about your age and smiling into the camera as she says, "*He* uses Natural Male Enhancement," immediately followed by an authoritative male warning byte: "SEEK IMMEDIATE HELP FOR AN ERECTION LASTING MORE THAN FOUR HOURS!"

You catch the eye of the bar-maid who reminds you of Gilgamesh's Divine Ale Wife, and you say, "Wouldn't happen here." She responds with a smile that is not quite sufficiently enigmatic so you decide to step out to the open-air tables in back for a cigarillo to recharge your respiratory apparatus. Beneath the sweltering August sky a wedding party is ranged around the tables, and as you look about for a place to sit, you spy yet another beautiful woman, a fortyish red head who is attached to the conference's host university. She is sitting with another younger male colleague who was once your student, and they motion you to join them. They are perhaps twenty years your junior but seem sincerely to want you to sit with them so you do. You cannot take your eyes off the woman whose face is smiling and bright as a new minted St. Gaudins gold piece but you make a point of looking from the one to the other as you speak with them, comparing life in the U.S. with life in Scandinavia where you have made your home for many years now. They tell you how puritanical America has become again as the three of you smoke and drink, and you speculate whether this delightful woman would ever consider the advantages of love with an older, shorter man who doesn't play tennis, but even well into the second round you manage to refrain from uttering that clownish question, fearing that anyway even if you did ask and even on the off-chance that she was interested you might wind up having to seek help for an erection that lasted more than four hours which no doubt is not all you might think it is cracked up to be.

These young colleagues insist on paying for both your doubles and you insist on paying for theirs or at least your own, and with her lovely fingers whose nails are the color of her hair, the gorgeous smiling red head stuffs your double sawbuck back into your shirt pocket, causing an involuntary tumescing of your left nipple as she tells you that the young man has covered the bill and refused to take the money from her.

Then she asks you to save a dance for her after the conference banquet, but you really do not see yourself inflicting your creaky old dude moves on her so you refer her to another colleague who has agreed to be your surrogate dancer this evening because you are at best awkward, and she looks into your eyes with her beautiful green ones and says that in her experience it's the guys who say they can't dance who are the most fun to cut the rug with, and you do not tell her that she does not understand that you are not a normal human being.

You cannot stop thinking about her lovely green eyes as you hoof it up the hill, deep August sweat wilting your freshly-donned raw-silk shirt, to the main house where the official conference banquet will be held, and along the way you meet a colleague who is the wife of a jazz guitarist, and she asks if you would like to nip out after dinner and before the dancing to catch his last set in a local jazz club. You would like that very much although you also think of a blue-eyed Italian woman named Carlita who was once your student and whose Sicilian profile has always enchanted you and who has told you she would be at the dinner tonight and asked you to save her a seat. Her face resembles a shy Nefertiti, and you would so very much like to kiss and touch that fabulous face or at least to have a heart-felt conversation with it in which your eyes would be allowed to meet her enchantingly level gaze, and she would occasionally touch your hand and arm and shoulder and back as is her wont, but at the same time you advise yourself not to be an asshole because she is more than twenty-five years younger than you. You should stick to girls your own old-dude age or even just one half-a-dozen years younger like Kristina the gorgeous Norwegian even though she is a triathlon participant in far better shape than you so you would be subjected to painful embarrassment if things went so far you would have to expose your naked body which would certainly be a flabby mortification compared to her long lean tanned one.

Nothing is simple, you think, as old O. Jones used to say when he attempted to waltz on the slippery rocks, and as you sweat your way up the last of the hill, and step into the vestibule of the conference building, perspiration stinging your eyes; you blink and see Carlita with her so gentle mild smile. She pours a blue-eyed glance slowly down your face which makes you clutch your heart and think, Could it be *me*, Carlita? Could *I* be the one? And you hear yourself thinking those romance-comic-book thoughts and understand in a flash of illumination that you are a male bimbo too old to fulfill the part as you pretend not to feast upon the blue light of her gaze and tell her about the jazz club and ask if she would care to join you.

She thinks for a moment, and then she says, "I would love to. Thank you for asking me," and you wonder why she had to think for a moment but nonetheless are very glad even though you remind yourself to remember that you are an old dude and that old dudes should leave young women in peace. You once saw Carlita, as you spoke with her in a conference room, lift her blue Italian eyes to observe a tall slim black-haired square-jawed young man who stepped in and you could so clearly read on her countenance the intensity of her interest in his body, in his being, and realized you were out of this, realized how pathetic it was that that should be a surprise, cautioned yourself to be content that she was talking to you at all and touching your hand and arm and shoulder and back on occasion to emphasize a point and make the contact of your words more physical as Italians do so well. You love that touchie-feelie shit. So listen to some jazz with her and go to bed early before you get so blotto that you disgrace yourself by thinking that you can fire off your cornball lines to these gorgeous women, making them think of you as a horny old creep who does not merit the time of day rather than a nice clean old fatherly dude, but you remind yourself that no one can really know what you are thinking and that you can't go to jail for thinking it either, although very possibly all these women know very well what all old dudes are thinking as surely as they can read the map of Ireland on your nose.

Nothing is simple, you think, and sin is behovely but all manner of thing could be quite okay if you but keep your neck in your pants as the father of a girlfriend once said when you were in the basement with her decades ago, and the father called down the basement stairs, What are you two doing down there, and she stopped kissing you long enough to say, We're necking, Pop, and he said, Well tell him to put his neck back in his pants and escort you upstairs.

Before the dinner tonight there are drinks on the grassy vast terrace, and everyone is dressed so nicely, and have you lost all sense of proportion you wonder, turning a tiny circle to be dazzled by one high-heeled beauty after another, and you step over to the Stoli-less bar where you have to settle for a glass of red wine, employing your Dean Swift line when the Divine Ale Wife fills the glass halfway; you ask her, "Pray tell, Madame, what is the function of the remainder of that glass," and she, prepared, retorts, "It is for the bouquet to blossom in, professor," and you, also prepared, tell her that since your sense of smell is in default she might as well fill it to the lip. She shoots you a skeptical look that quickly evolves into a friendly glance, and you compliment her pouring technique as her cute wrist turns to tip the bottle over your glass and complete the job, and you go off swilling wine and glad-handing the conference attendees, one of whom you spoke to the evening before in a rather blunt manner and therefore must take extra care to be certain she does not think you dislike her when it was only an excess of vodka that made you misgauge your repartee.

So you kiss her hand with an elaborate application of your lips, even though a gentleman never actually kisses a woman's hand but only holds it in his and kisses his own thumb, murmuring, "Enchanté, Madame," and she replies in classic New Yorkese, "You are so fulla shit but I have already forgiven you," and you happily smooch her hand again – a nice hand! – and say with real sincerity, "Your servant, Madame! Your liege!"

Then you are called in to the dining hall and the white-clothed tables and crested plates and cutlery and tented linen napkins, and there are speeches and more wine, and you step out back to smoke, and a lovely black woman you used to work with asks you for a cigarillo, and you say something or other that gets your face close to hers, and she lets you kiss her, but you note distantly now that you are experiencing a bit of tunnel vision and you realize that you are in danger of having one of these nights that occur perhaps twice a year where your short term memory will be seriously compromised, and you will wake next morning with only the patchiest recollection of how the evening ensued, how you got home or got to bed or how badly you slurred or staggered or even, as happens once every three years or so, whether you actually took a flop, and previously you would worry that you might have done terrible things during the blank patches of time where your memory was scratched out, but it seems you never did, or at least no one ever kicked in your door next day to beat you up or lynch you or arrest you so you figure probably your ethics are deeply enough entrenched in your spinal column that you can continue to maintain the human potentialist mantra of I'm okay-You're okay though still you are unclear whether tomorrow you will have to apologize to the black woman for kissing her out back although she did seem to like it and did not resist at all, and it was really nice.

But then the dinner is over and you are in a car with Carlita and the jazz guitarist's wife, headed to the club, and you take the back seat, a perfect vantage point from which to study the elegant neck and profile of Carlita, and from somewhere inside the sparkling ball of confusion that is your mind, the sparkles being brief points of profound lucidity, you sternly caution yourself to do all in your power not to make Carlita unhappy.

Then the three of you are entering the New Montmartre Jazz House and are seated around a table ten feet from the quintet who are doing a wonderfully wicked version of Miles's "Topaz," and you realize what a privilege it is to be here in this little club with such great musicians and two beautiful women and a double Stoli which could more accurately be called a quadruple and hearing those lovely sour trumpet notes and the cool cool cool fucking guitar, and you are hoping that Carlita enjoys the music, and then there is another quadruple Stoli in your glass, and the Chinese woman named Jin who owns the club comes over to the table to say hello and addresses you as "Dr." which in theory you are, having a Ph.D. on some marginal creative topic you used to know something about thirty years ago, but you feel so goddamned good there is no reason to elaborate, and you notice Carlita's gorgeous blue Sicilian eyes taking you in, and their expression is so warm that you decide that your next drink should be a glass of ice water to slow your progress toward oblivion but you forget and order a double quadruple Stoli because the guitar player is doing such a cool run on "Sienna" so you realize that you are not likely to avoid a vodka blitz in the not too distant future, and then the three of you are back in the car, returning to the dinner where people are dancing and congregated out on the grassy terrace where your good colleague Bob Giangrando with his warmly sardonic smile and cool understated voice says, "I have some shit you have *got* to sample," and then a very young very pretty very innocent-looking woman with black hair and blue eyes behind black-framed glasses hands you a very well packed bong, and you draw the hot smooth skunk into your throat, thinking "Holy fuckin' mackerel!" or maybe actually saying it , and at one and the same time it seems to you that all is lost and all is gained as your brain wraps around the cooling-down August heat on that grassy terrace, and a mosquito lands on the back of your hand and you bemusedly watch as it sips some of your blood and *why not, little lady, why not?* you think, as Bob Giangrando pats your back and smiles a smile you might think sinister except that you know it is a sweet smile and the very young very innocent-looking very pretty woman with black hair and blue eyes is packing another bong, but you suddenly realize that Carlita is nowhere in sight, and you are ready to propose marriage to her, and maybe you say that aloud because the very young very pretty very innocent-looking black-haired woman with heartbreaking blue jeans says, "I'll marry you. Why not? You could be my first husband." And she chuckles sweetly as you think, or maybe say, that is the kind of hyperbole that will help you make it through another winter of your discontent, and you wonder if you could get away with kissing her, but you have got to find Carlita so you venture in to the ballroom where everyone is dancing.

    This is a very very dangerous place for you to be where someone might suggest cutting the rug with you, and if you say yes, and how can you not? you are in danger of taking a record-breakingly long Charlie Chaplin stagger halfway across the floor so you just stand at the door opening, and you see Carlita dancing in such a way that if you were the kind of a guy who *could* do so, *would* weep because she is doing some kind of a middle-eastern dance with her arms and hands extended and wrists turning, and your heart opens as you realize that you will never live long enough to see her grow old which means her beauty for you is immortal but also that she might well be around to see you turn into an ancient fossil, and you are stricken by the understanding that your life is over, that this Sicilian beauty has a whole life before her that does not include you, and with that understanding you take a step sidewise to right your faltering balance and fortunately there is a wall there that you stumble into rather than taking a header onto the floor, and as you hang against the door jamb, you realize that it is time for you to go home but that you will in no way be able to negotiate the steep hill down to the official conference hotel rooms so you remain hanging there, hoping that your balance will suddenly, miraculously replenish itself and allow you the possibility of gathering what dignity you might have left to depart in a straight-enough line that no one will notice you or see you stagger disgracefully, and then for some obscure reason, you get the idea of mouthing a quote from "Under Milkwood," and you do that.

Pronouncing the words in the best stentorian splendor you can evoke, you proclaim, "Mr. Thomas: Is going to be sick!"

Apparently you say that loudly enough during a pause in the music that heads turn toward you, including Carlita's lovely Sicilian face, and then she is there in front of you peering with concern into what could only be the smudge of your puss.

"Are you all right?" she asks.

With some difficulty, you manage to say, "I think it is time for me to return to my room."

And that beautiful woman smiles at you the mildest of smiles and asks, "May I walk with you?" Even fogged as you are, you do not fail to recognize the elegant discretion of her wording. She might have said, "Would you like me to help you?" Or "Let me help you." Or even, "You can't make it alone." But no, she said, "May I walk with you?"

And you reply, "I should be very honored and pleased indeed if you would walk with me, Ms. Carlita."

The walk is not among the moments of greatest dignity of your life. You need to be held tightly under your arm, but Carlita does it with gentle firmness, her warm body snug against yours, and in no time you are down the hill, and you only drop your room key three times before you manage to open the door and concentrate on asking without a slur, "Would you like to come in for a nightcap?"

To which she replies, miraculously, "Yes." She lisps the word slightly. Not a full lisp. Not "Yeth," but more a slight shade of "Yesh."

And then in no time at all, the two of you are seated closely on your sofa, and you are thinking, Am I really going to get this lucky? Aloud you say: "Carlita: May I kiss you?"

"Yesh."

And you do that. Several times in succession. With great reverence and tenderness but increasing intensity. And you touch her lovely face with your fingertips to which she responds by closing her eyes and smiling with heart-breaking sweetness, moving her face in to catch your touches, and you know you don't deserve to be so happy, old profligate that you are, but you will take this good fortune and let it flood your ageing pump, but then you say something you should not say.

You say, "How can you let an old guy like me kiss you?"

To which she replies the only sensible thing. "Why don't you shut up and just kiss me."

And you do that. You kiss her lips and her face and her eyes and her neck. You sigh with mighty pleasure and look and look into her baby blues and see beneath her gaze a certain sadness, sad but smiling and so very blue, and you whisper, "You are so beautiful," to which she replies, "Thank you," in such a sweet breathy whisper, and you say, "I have been crazy about you since the first moment I saw you."

She answers nothing, only looks into your eyes with her unblinking so-blue gaze, and in that moment you come to an understanding of passion's failure. There is no way that you would ever, even in your youth, be able to implement the fulfillment of your veneration of her beauty, your wish, your desire, your hunger to become part of her and for her to become part of you. The joining of bodies is only a symbol of what we so fervently wish we could, but never can. Even joined we look across a chasm at one another. And so you merely whisper, "Let's go to bed," and she whispers back, "Okay," and that whispered word on its way to reaching you has touched every part of her sweet mouth and moves toward your face, moist from her tongue, a gift wrapped in her sweet gin-scented breath.

There is no way, after all the vodka, that you dare ingest any Natural Male Enhancement so you need have no fear of an erection that lasts for more than four seconds even, but do your very best with the organs at your command to give her some pleasure at least and perhaps you do manage for you are rewarded with breathy sounds of joy and desperate sighs and you hope that she is truly pleased but what the hell, what can you do but your best, and you are just so bloody goddamn glad – so glad! – to be naked in bed with this lovely naked woman; even if nothing further ever comes of it, this is a moment in your life that time can never reclaim, and you are murmuring a hymn of admiration into the warm cherry-red cup of her ear as you reverently caress everything of her you can reach and tell her again you have been mad about her since the moment you first saw her, and perhaps you are gushing but there is a definite core of molten truth to your words, perhaps you could almost even call it love, but you manage to avoid that word with its four-lettered landscape of traps and springs, and though you wonder if she is skeptical because she says nothing, and you wonder if you understand the nature of your meeting, perhaps a woman of her age in this young century considers this a simple casual encounter, but you cannot consider this casual by any means, you are thrilled, you are wild about her and you see again that perhaps you are nothing but an elderly male bimbo or a self-deceived jerk, but what in the world matters at all beyond that this beautiful woman has allowed you to kiss her and she is here and naked and allowing you to touch and admire the beauty of her with all your senses and none of this would have happened if you had not gone through this day following each and every step that led you to this glorious series of moments, and in five-ten-twenty years at most, you will be in the house which none leave who have entered it, at the end of the road from which there is no way back, to the house wherein the dwellers are bereft of light, where dust is their drink and clay their meat, and they see no light, wrapped about as they are in darkness.

But not yet. Not yet. And you turn your eyes once more to the mild unblinking gaze of this lovely 21st century Italian Nefertiti, and what could you ever have said to this rare good moment of fortune but yes.

OLD DUDE IN THE FREE STATE

"I would love to kiss you.
The price of kissing is your life.
Now my loving is running toward my life shouting,
What a bargain, let's buy it!"

- Rumi (translation by Coleman Barks)

You roam the Free State with your buddy, F, who knows a barmaid at Nemoland, and she has promised him a free drink. You don't need a free drink, but you want to meet the barmaid. Barmaids are mythic. You can never know too many barmaids. Turns out you meet four, and one is prettier than the other, and they all have the same name – Annemethe. F introduces you to *his* Annemethe, whose daughter is in school with *his* daughter. She's cute. She's thirty-two. She pops two cold bottles of Free State beer and pours two shots of bitter schnapps. The air is redolent of the sweet seductive smell of skunk. The two of you chat with Annemethe, but it's a busy night. She doesn't have time. You drink up to move on, and Annemethe comes out from behind the bar to embrace F, then takes your hand in both of hers and pours you a smile that warms your ancient heart.

It is mid-September, the kind of lingering summer night where the air is laden with the promise of autumnal dying, the time of year that Rilke spoke of:

> *Whoever has no house now, will never have one.*
> *Whoever is alone will stay alone,*
> *will sit, read, write long letters throughout the evenings*
> *and wander on the boulevards, up and down,*
> *restlessly, while the dry leaves are blowing.*

But you are an optimistic old dude. Two nights ago you went to the theater, and the actress doing the *Shirley Valentine* monologue suddenly put your full name right in the middle of it, and when you heard your name there it made you question the soundness of your mind, but she told you afterwards that she had seen you coming in and that was her way of saying hello. This has put a gloss on your feel-good shield, and now you are loose in the Free State with your buddy F, who at fifty-five is ten years your junior.

As the two of you walk on the dark dirt paths studded with burning barrels and hash stalls and milling Friday-nighters, F says, "You know, I met a girl the other day who is almost twenty-five years younger than me, but I can see the way she looks at me that she thinks we could be together. She has a kid, I have a kid, we're both alone. But I think she's afraid. I think she sees me as an intellectual, and she only went to ninth grade.!"

"You could teach her," you say. "She might just be longing for an intellectual guy to help her learn how to read a poem, look at a painting, know what to think about a short story."

You can see F is tempted. You step into the Woodstock bar, order two Free State beers and sit at the tables outside amidst the smoke-eaters and unruly dogs of all sizes and quarelling Inuits. There's an agreeable chill to the dark, and you tell F about the woman you met in Manhattan, the Signora, who is nearly thirty years younger than yourself but roused you from spiritual sleep with her kiss a few weeks ago. A mystery; but how could you say other than yes to a beautiful young poet who consented to come to your hotel room and allowed you to seduce her. "If she lived here instead of the other side of the ocean, and if she would have an old dude like me, I'd take a chance on her in a minute. Maybe it would only work for a couple years. Five at most maybe. Then I start to fall apart. But five years of joy is five years of joy compared to five years of writing long letters and walking up and down the boulevards."

But she doesn't live here. So what you have with her is long letters and two or three meetings a year. You'll take it.

F replenishes the beers and tells about a woman he met a few months before, a dancer. "She was beautiful, I tell you she was beautiful. I took her home."

"You took her home?"

"I took her home. We drank a bottle of wine. We started doing what men and women sometimes do. I opened another bottle of wine, and she started telling me about a problem she has with her toenails. Chronic fungus. Here's this beautiful naked woman on my sofa, music on the stereo, an open bottle of wine. But I kept thinking about toenail fungus. I couldn't get past it."

"You could have put a pair of socks on her. Look past the toes. Remember Schade's poem about the Finnish girl with bad teeth who showed him her breasts."

F laughs loud. "Yeah, we've got to focus on the positive." He thinks for a moment. "But you know, women look differently at men than men look at women. Men look at women in parts, women see the whole man. They see us holistically."

"Wouldn't it be pretty to think so?" you say.

The two of you are sitting alone at a picnic table in the dark, and three young women approach and ask in English if they can take the empty seats.

"It would be an honor," you say.

"Well," says F with a smile, "Let's see what it would be before making pronouncements about it."

In Danish you remind him about the saying of the High One that admonishes to remember always to praise the beauty of a woman, for he who praises sometimes gets.

The young women are speaking English – American as the Danes say. There is a blond with clear plastic eyeglasses and full lips, a brunette who looks vaguely like Sarah Palin, and another brunette who has the sleeves of her blouse pulled down over her delicate shapely hands, something you have never been able to resist. You wonder how women figure out that something like that would reach right into a man's heart, wonder whether they devise such practices or whether it is just that you are a susceptible old dude who can't resist anything about women.

You ask, "Are you girls from Scarsdale?" because the blond reminds you a little of the Signora, who is from Scarsdale. They're not, but the question is sufficiently stupid to get you all chatting. They are from Oregon, are in Denmark for a graduate program in urban planning. The one with the shapely hands is Emily, originally from Vermont, and her brown eyes make you clutch your heart. The blond is named Lou Anne Leapingdeer.

"Leapingdeer?!"

"It's an Americanization of the German name, *Hirschsprung*."

You show her that very name, Hirschprung, on your little tin box of mini-cigars, and the two of you marvel at the smallness of the world. Emily excuses herself and disappears, to your considerable disappointment, but Lou Anne and Sarah Palin reassure you she will be back. She's just gone to buy some space cookies. Lou Anne says they spoke with a dealer earlier who was trying to court Emily by doing things like giving her a lighter for her joint which was a novelty lighter – gave her a shock. Then he touched her hand with an electric fly swatter – another shock. You are thinking how if you got the opportunity you would shock her with gentle touches of veneration, but then maybe that's not the sort of shock she prefers.

Your plan is to go to the Free State JazzKlub, and F, God bless him, handsome fellow that he is, says, "Why don't you girls join us?"

To your surprise they are enthusiastic. Lou Anne tells you there will be blue grass in the JazzKlub tonight. She tells you that she heard the group playing last night right here in the Woodstock. She tells you it was music that touched her heart deeply. You were thinking you wanted to hear some jazz, but are not averse to hearing blue grass that touched deep into Lou Anne's blond heart with her full lips and clear plastic spectacles and blue eyes that make you think of the Signora.

Emily returns with her space cookies in a plastic bag, and the five of you head along Pusher Street to the JazzKlub, but at the door the girls hang back. The Sarah Palin one says, "There's smoke in there."

You tell her that second-hand smoke can make you feel good. F says, "Not much hope for a place to go in the Free State if you can't take the smoke."

By now you've paid your eight bucks admission, had your hand stamped and bought two bottles of Free State beer, and you and F sit alone at a table while the musicians set up: two electric hardbody guitars, drums, a keyboard, and a guy with an alto sax. Doesn't look like blue grass.

You ask F, "Why did the girls leave us? We were perfect for them."

F shares your surprise. "You're right. We were perfect for them."

The JazzKlub looks like an agreeably dingy Third World café, with mismatched furniture and gouged walls. On a table is a flower display in the shape of a tenor sax, commemorating the recently deceased St. Louis jazz man Luther Thomas, who had lived for years in the Free State. Dead at 59. Would've been six years ago for you. Silently you thank your body for plodding on.

Then you light a little cigar and swig your beer from the bottle and look up, startled to see an incredibly beautiful raven-haired woman walking toward your table on high-heeled boots. F stands and greets her, and they kiss. On the mouth. Lingeringly. He introduces you as a famous writer – the hyperbole of a supportive friend – and you say, "Not nearly as famous as F." They step aside and chat and when F returns, alone, he says, "That's her. With the toe fungus."

"Oh maan. Not all the toe fungus in the world could nullify that beauty."

"Yeah, but I couldn't."

"Even when you can't, there's other stuff to do."

A passing black man does a double take at you. It is Henri, a clarinetist who occasionally has backed you up at poetry readings. He has a look of dismay on his face as he reaches to hug you and thump your back. "I hear you and Bodil split?"

"Shit happens."

"Couples like you and Bodil are not supposed to split!"

"Shit happens."

Then he is gone, and F looks suddenly to the bar. "They're back!" he says, and you see the slender sauntering figures of Lou Anne and Emily approaching your table, bearing bottles of Free State beer. What a good old life this is, you think, marveling that all it takes to make you happy is to be in the presence of beauty. Turns out they ditched Sarah Palin. They settle at your and F's table, and the jazz begins, and the alto goes straight into your blood, and you share a mini-cigar with Emily, delivering and receiving it to and from her shapely hand, as you watch an extremely large African-American woman dancing like a mobilized Niki de Saint Phalle sculpture, like the Venus of Willendorf gone jazz-rhythmic, and her beauty, the beauty of her moves, is overwhelming. A voice from behind you, a woman leaning close, says softly, "I'd like to dance, too. You look like you might be a good dancer."

"I'm not," you apologize, "but thank you for wanting me to be. In fact, F is my surrogate dancer. You'll have to speak with him," but F is in deep conversation with Lou Anne. He looks up to say to you in Danish, "Lou Anne is twenty-nine!"

"Yeah, that can work – you're only fifty-five," you reply in Danish, cautioning yourself to keep things in proportion, not to be a foolish old dude, but the alto is so bloody beautiful, you are grooving at the core of your heart, and then you and Emily are outside in the dark sharing a cigar-sized skunk joint that she produced from her bag. Two hits and you are there in that other world where everything slows to such a perfect pace and the decelerated moments present themselves in passing for a thorough examination, each and every one of them, before flowing on, and the face of Emily touches deep in that region where the alto has prepared a place for it, as your mind sorts through options, and your superego admonishes you to maintain what is left of your balance and remember that you are truly an old dude more than twice her age.

Emily tells you she is leaving for Berlin early in the a.m., and it is already early in the a.m., and she says she would like to read one of your books, and you give her your "*Flaneur, Plongeur*" business card with your email address and ask her to write and tell you how she liked Berlin, and she says that she will, that that will give her something to look forward to about going home to Oregon, and water stings your old-fool eyes, and your faces are so close that you are in danger of offering a fatal kiss but manage to restrain yourself, reasoning that a kiss, if accepted, would be awfully nice, but also, if rebuffed, could ruin the loveliness of this entire encounter, so you are about to instead recite a poem by Rumi, but then remember that it begins, "I would love to kiss you," and that really will not do, so you only take the joint from her cute fingers, two more tokes, and she takes two more, and then the two of you are back in the Klub, and the keyboard man is playing wild percussions on his tangents while the alto wails a sound that finger fucks heaven, and you are wondering whether you should have just taken the chance and kissed her anyway, but also thinking what a privilege it is to sit in this little Klub hearing such magnificent sounds, and you are about as high as a man can get and still remain upright and somewhat rational, and then you notice that you are not just thinking these things, you are in fact making an oral presentation of them to the two young women who are listening attentively, perhaps only politely, or perhaps memerized by your stupidity, and you are wondering just how much you may have told them about your private thoughts, maybe you spilled the whole beans, but then you think well what's wrong with forthrightness and honesty anyway, and F is swaying to the music, his eyes closed, and you look at your watch and see it is half past two and time for old dudes to be in bed.

You say your farewells, and Emily hops from her chair and hugs you tight, and you say, "Uhmmm…" and she says again that she will write and that she wants to read one of your books, and you are moved right down to the elastic of your sock-holders, although you know full well that she will not write, and why should she?

You float through the night-dark unpaved Free State streets, congratulating yourself on having succeeded for once in not making a total ass of yourself, though wondering whether in fact you did, or whether you should have, as you pass dark clusters of people who in another world might seem threatening but who here are simply other people in the dark of the night pursuing happiness.

On the other side of the gate, back in the real world, a Mercedes taxi waits to drive you along the canals of Christiania, over Knippels Bridge, black water glistening below, through the deserted center of the ancient kingdom, and back to your little cobblestoned street where you let yourself in to your little apartment and stand on your Persian carpet, cheered to be surrounded by the art you have spent the past couple of decades collecting. You turn a circle, gazing from picture to picture, the colorist Skotte Olsen with his strange oil faces of peering eyes, Barry Lereng Wilmont's gouaches of Dan Turèll motifs, Savino's eerie disembodied souls wafting through the canvases, Teodor Bok's strange angels…

Then you light a little cigar and open your computer to see if, perchance, there is a message from the Signora, and there is! And then you are glad you didn't kiss anybody tonight, although the Signora probably wouldn't mind, even if you wish she *did* mind, at least a little, but it is nice to have a woman to be faithful to, even if there is no reason at all for you to be, and as always when you see her name lit up in the inbox, your heart goes pit a pat because there is no way around it, you *are* an old fool. It is just a couple of lines: "My dear Professore," she begins, as she always begins her mails to you, and tells how the past couple of days have been so full of demands that she has been unable to write but wanted to assure you that she is thinking of you and is sending kisses and will have time tomorrow to write a good long mail, and your elation is mixed with apprehension that it would be so easy to misunderstand what "kisses" and "thinking of you" really mean. But she did say she wanted to "assure" you, so it is hard not to think she didn't mean those kisses to be actual kisses, even romantic ones perhaps, and those thoughts of you to be warm ones, and so what if you are pathetic, you like feeling these emotions, they make you feel alive.

Then you are in your bed, which is a row boat without oars or anchor, floating away, a smile on your face, and you think that if the inevitable surprise should come for you in your sleep tonight, it will have been a good old life; what better way to go than assured that you are safe in the Signora's thoughts?

I AM A SLAVE
TO THE NUDITY OF WOMEN
───────

> "I do not know with what resolve
> I could stand against it, a naked woman
> Asking of me anything."
>
> Alberto Ríos
> *Teodoro Luna's Two Kisses*

He sits on his sofa, vodka close to hand, a book of poetry open on his lap, although he is not reading. He is ruminating, and he advises himself not to think about rising to step into his office to check the full-screen laptop opened on his desk to see if the e-mail inbox is illuminated with the name of Lucia. Yet he does rise, the book closed around one finger, does step into his office and does look at the laptop screen and sees that there is no illuminated Lucia there and tells himself, Well *that* is no doubt *that*.

    Did you think, he thinks, that the two of you were in love, could be in love? She is so much younger and lives so far away. And he who had always been suspicious of that word until Eileen made him see, or believe, it could be possible and then proceeded to withdraw from a love she had encouraged him to believe was life-long? Still staring at the screen of the laptop, he thinks how all certainties he had once felt about the idea of love, both negative and positive, were now tipped over; the only certainty remaining concerns "chemistry." You know, he thinks, and have always known that "the chemistry" has to be right, and what *is* the chemistry. Lucia has the right chemistry, but what *is* that chemistry? Her gentle, kind smile. Her blue eyes, tender and sad and merry, yes. Her face, yes. Her body, its lines and curves and fullnesses and hollows. Her rump – how odd, he thinks, his heart captured by a rump. And the character in her chin – yet he has known people with receding chins who had character nonetheless–the features of a face deceive so why does a certain face make you see possibilities, feel that happiness is possible, trust. Yet there is no denying the chemistry of her face or her body. Or, for that matter, the chemistry of her intellect, the way she is able to see things, surprise him with a word of understanding, yes, so chemistry is more than the arrangement of features of a face and a body and a rump. Could he ever love a woman, at least initially, whose rump did not win him? And it is not even a specific kind or shape or size of rump but a rump that, well, makes him follow it. And what does that say about him as a human being? He finds it difficult to believe that he is standing there, disappointed, and thinking these things. Lucia is so different from Eileen yet he cannot deny that he "loved" Eileen and is on his way to "loving" Lucia (under Eileen's tutelage he had removed the quotation marks from the word "love" – now they are back in place for he realizes he does not know what "love" might be).

There is, of course, he thinks then, something more: The way she looks at him with admiration sparkling in her eyes; the admiring things she says. He realizes that he is a sucker for that.

This is ridiculous, he thinks.

He returns to the sofa and sips his vodka and looks at the book of poetry, a slender volume whose slenderness seems somehow to promise disproportionate depth and breadth. Still he does not read. He stares at the page and thinks.

He thinks maybe it was that Eileen, with her long chestnut hair and perfect lips and tenderness and appealing femininity (or was that an act?), kicked him out, surprising him when he still loved her by revealing that she no longer loved him, so that he still had his heart open, even though his pride or self-respect would never allow him to beg or even try to convince her of the genuineness of his love for her (he believed at that time, for a time, that he knew what genuine love was) – he thinks maybe it is for these reasons that he is ready, even eager, to love again or to keep loving for as long as he can, specifically to see if what he feels for Lucia and she for him might be love, because when he loves (regardless of what love may or may not be), he feels almost complete, so it is no good to be alone again as he was before he met Eileen, even though he was fairly content being alone for those few years, probably because, before that, for the last ten years of his marriage to Jessica, he did not love her at all, but only *tended* the relationship in a somewhat cynical manner, trying to avoid things that annoyed her, and there were so many things that annoyed her (to name but one, she would not go to the movies with him, an activity he had always enjoyed, because she so loathed the prospect of people munching candy in the dark), trying not to do things that would make her unhappy while simultaneously trying not to make himself unhappy.

Finally, of course, he failed at both things, made both of them unhappy, just as she had done (if she was to blame at all, though it takes two to tango and so forth) because, he suspected, of the basic lack of love in the relationship – (relationship, he thinks, what a clunky word! And of course, he thinks, what *is* love anyway, etc., although the love he felt for Eileen, in contrast to his feeling for Jessica, left him no doubt, though that lack of doubt reminded him of the necessity of maintaining a certain healthy skepticism about it all) – and therefore was not unhappy being alone, even though at times he was lonely, but there was the occasional woman (even if sex without love was ultimately unsatisfying, yet sex when it's bad is not so very bad, although it can be absolutely dismal to wake alongside another human being you do not love but whose body cavities, to put it hyperbolically crudely, you have merely made use of and so forth).

But then there was Eileen with her long auburn hair and delicate hands and beautiful mouth and feminine manner who told him he was the love of her life, winning him over by the force of her conviction that love clearly did exist, and she really did seem to love him to the extent that he actually began to understand that he did not love himself, but then in fact *began* to love himself, and then to love her, in the way a man can only love a woman when he genuinely has learned, preferably from her, to love himself (all these things, of course, being postulates built upon postulates when you have never in the first place answered the question of what, after all, *is* love, etc.) and there was the rub perhaps because just about when he began to love himself, and thus her, and began to think *she* was the love of *his* life, it seemed, she began to grow increasingly bored or annoyed with him (*Do you have to crunch your cornflakes like that?* kind of thing and so forth), ultimately showing him the door and giving him a verbal nudge toward it.

The mental image of him being nudged toward the door, though not precisely what happened, merely a manner of thinking, arrests him. He does not wish to think about these things, this recent history of his life. Living alone in his new apartment, small and lightless as it was in the depth of winter, as he negotiated the unexpected loss of Eileen, he began to be plagued by erotic fantasies of pain and humiliation that first repulsed, then baffled, then began to seem the inevitable next step for him to entertain and embrace. So he made a place for them in his psyche and allowed them to play out on the screen of his consciousness. Where, he wondered, were these scenes occurring? In what dimension did Eileen smile at him with such refined cruelty, laughing at his pain and him laughing along with her and taking pleasure from it all? Did he really entertain such thoughts? In what dimension did he welcome that cruelty? Perhaps he had thought (or convinced himself) that this entertainment would progress to some manner of release and perhaps it did on some level but on some other, perhaps more important level, he felt it involved an adulterating of what he had thought of as the closest he had come to a real experience of love, while at the same time realizing that this might all along have been the deeper point of all this, his imagined surrender to her imaginary cruelty, but no, no, no, you are confused, why would cruelty suddenly come into it when what had attracted them to one another was a mutual empathy and tenderness?

And he understands then that his intellect is limited such that he is capable of conjuring this cacophony of possibilities but not of organizing them in a comprehensible manner. Part of it has to do with the relationship of loss and lust but what is the nature of that relationship? The question makes his skull ache.

He looks at his drink and thinks, *Vodka: it keepeth the reason from stifling*, and sips, sips again, returns his attention to the open book in his lap where he reads, "I am a slave to the nudity of women…" The line takes his breath away, and he looks up from the page to contemplate those words. His eyes come to rest on a painting of an angel on the wall. The angel is slouched gloomily at a dining table before an empty plate and empty glass. Somehow the angel seems related to the line of poetry he has just read, which evokes the nudity of Lucia. He tells himself not to, but does lay the open book face down on the sofa cushion and does rise to go into the office to check the computer: No illuminated Lucia in the inbox. Of course. That *is* it. His vodka is empty so he throws two more cubes into the glass and pours in five fingers, returns to the sofa and picks up the book from the cushion, but a new thought strikes him:

That in the beginning, the very beginning, Eileen might have feared him and might have *wanted* to fear him and possibly confused fear with respect, confused that force she perceived in him, that she feared, with masculinity and possibly needed to have that illusion of him as forceful and masculine and fear-inspiring, which he never thought of himself as or even wanted to pretend to be, but perhaps was unconsciously inspired to do by a subliminal perception of and response to her fear, which caused an erotic reaction at that level, for he does recall how aroused he had been by her femininity, that she was small and slight and slender, that she seemed to enjoy cooking for him, even *serving* him, seemed to expect him to make demands of her, to seduce and undress her, to trap her wrists in his one hand as the other had its way with her body while her eyes met his in what appeared a kind of blissful surrender. Suddenly this appears to him as though illuminated along with the suspicion or perhaps understanding that it was the wearing away of her illusion that had led her to grow discontent with him and to the termination of their erotic life together.

Of course, he thinks, you have to realize that the fucking was important, and neither was the lack of fucking unimportant after she began to grow disenchanted with him. In the beginning, the fucking was the sine qua non and be-all-end-all, etc., a mix of instinct and consideration, of giving and holding back, of urgency tempered by reserve, spiced by the discovery and revelation of mutual secrets. But Eileen was also sometimes the aggressor in their erotic play, she was good at aggressing, was it a mistake for him not to have resisted, not to have kept her in that place where her illusion of him could thrive, but he didn't, he even discussed it (*How did you know I would like it if you did that?* and so forth), should have kept it pure of words, but he didn't, until there weren't many secrets left (there are always secrets, etc., no one can ever truly know another or even, perhaps especially, him- or herself, etc.) which led to a nakedness that went beyond the physical to the spiritual, the psychological, to what seemed to be a complete nakedness in their embrace but maybe just was based on that mutual feminine-masculine illusion so that they were building on an illusion, an unsound basis for love, which at first seemed akin to some kind of state of grace, to know and to be known (insofar as one can ever know or be known and so forth), to know another with reverence for the knowledge, to be known with tenderness for your vulnerabilities and so on and so forth.

Then came the moment when one or the other of them, both perhaps, used the knowledge without care, teasingly, took the gloves off. I-*know*-you kind of thing. I see right through you, and so forth, and Ha ha, you'd probably actually *like* that, *how pathetic* kind of thing. And then one or the other of them feels they're out on thin ice and in for a dunking from which he or she will emerge shivering and distraught. Or maybe the shadow part which was revealed is simply now illuminated, out in the light, and no longer has the force it had when it was locked away (you are, after all, what you are kind of thing), no longer interesting, or maybe just an illusion, self-knowledge being a series of lost self-deceptions and knowledge of the other being a series of disenchantments perhaps, the shadow of desire being dissipated in the light of awareness, and perhaps after that, perhaps when you get to that point, the beauty of real desire is possible, if by then you have any measure of desire left at all, but what it all led to finally was that he was no longer the love of her life, although she was still the love of his or seemed so (assuming that love is a real quantity or quality at all and not merely an illusion that each human being freely embraces because of his or her incompleteness.)

Or maybe, he thinks, it's just a matter of all passion eventually burning out regardless of what you do. Time limited. Or familiarity breeds contempt kind of thing. Desire an illusion as well as love, etc., on the other side of which is the cooling.

But, he thinks, Eileen reached the cooling before he did. As far as he knows he might never have reached the cooling, although it is entirely possible that his love was perversely stoked to even greater life by her cooling, that his desire began to flourish more greatly in panic at the withdrawal of hers. Too late to know now, for now he is irrevocably separated from her and does not want to return, could not, even if she wanted him to, even if she implored him, that would only embarrass him on her behalf.

But his heart is still open to love ("love").

However, the chemistry has to be right. He can't just love any woman. The chemistry is right with Lucia, but is that a chemistry of passion which is also doomed to burn out? (And, again, of course, what is at the root of this *right chemistry* business is quite another question; it seems there are only questions upon questions and perhaps the only way out is to become a Buddhist and renounce all desire as illusion, but who in the world other than a damn Buddhist wants to live without desire, to ignore the jumping of your blood when it jumps; even if its jumping is only delusive, it does, in fact, jump, and that must be the bottom line: your blood jumps. *His* blood jumps, although perhaps one should seek a state of unjumping blood, the age of calm and wise blood, where a man and a woman live together beyond passion just as companions of different sexes without sex, How was your day kind of thing, And how was *yours*, etc., but would that really mean no more fucking at all forever; even if it is *but a tingling of the nerves* kind of thing, he does not wish to contemplate the entire rest of his life without it. And it is no mere tingling of the nerves, the dance to orgasm is surely sacred, or is that so much eyewash dispersed for profit by New Age and advertising mountebanks. We are in the dark, he thinks; *I* am in the dark. And there is another possible aspect to this chemistry business. What if the so-called "right chemistry" is in fact an unconscious formula devised by a variety of subliminal experiences and forces that has become his destiny merely because, say, his mother once looked at him in a certain way when his father had said or done something or other at a time when he was pre- or semi-lingual which then programmed his desire in a direction quite beyond his control or comprehension so that when the "right chemistry" presents itself, it merely turns him into a "fool for love" or as Milton put it, *Among them Hee a spirit of frenzy sent who hurt their minds/and sent them in a mad fury to hasten their destruction* or something like that, which could conceivably mean that when he longs to "love" a certain woman what he really longs for is to reinvent Eden and then the inevitable Fall from Grace, his own destruction or, to put it less melodramatically, his own nonproductive infatuation – a repetition of failure?)

Nonetheless, his heart was still open to love, it seems to him, after Eileen stopped loving him and he met Lucia and felt the first stirrings of love which led to the two of them putting their mouths together and intertwining their tongues and tasting one another's saliva which, though objectively might seem repellent, was subjectively quite stimulating -- Wow indeed! -- as was tasting and touching virtually all other parts of her body.

Actually, he knew Lucia already for the past couple of years, but never dreamed she was interested in him love-wise because she is so much younger than he, and anyway, when he met her he had just been taught by Eileen to love himself, and was not even thinking of Lucia in that way, being as he was so "fully in love" with Eileen, although apparently she, Lucia, was thinking of him in that way to his great surprise, and now he sees suddenly, as though scales have fallen from his eyes as it says in the Bible or somewhere, that he desires her also, in fact very much so. And what, he wonders, is the essence of his desire for Lucia? Surprise, perhaps? Surprise she would even for an instant desire him? There was so much against it. He is eighteen years older than she for one thing, lives two thousand miles away, and each of them has a life there, where he or she lives, from which they neither can nor wish to extricate themselves.

He thinks back over the girls and women he has been with over the six decades of his life – well, the five erotically active decades – and can only conclude that of the ten or twelve, he has only *approached* what he would think of as love (if he had a definition) with the two: Jessica, to whom he was married for twenty years, and that love, if it had ever really been love ("love" which has still not been explicated) burned out in the first ten, even eight years; and Eileen, who taught him really to love, or so it seemed, and then, after fifteen years, rather abruptly gave him the boot, and now perhaps his passion for Lucia, too, was already at an end, or rather hers for him.

Now he is sixty-three (Liar! You're sixty-five!) and hardly wiser about these things than he was at fourteen, albeit with a more complex confusion, and now is involved with Lucia whom he feels he could love, maybe already does love – (if he is not merely setting traps of illusion for himself, falling for women with whom his relationship [relationship, what a word!] is by definition doomed and perishable [which is of course a real possibility – cf. Milton's *spirit of frenzy* etc.], although he cannot deny that he becomes extremely glad every time he sees or even imagines her face and her body and her kind and gentle manner as well as her wit and intelligence [blood jumping and so forth], and of course her rump, and who seems quite definitely to find something of value in him which tends to make him value himself--cf., Gene Kelly in some musical romantic comedy singing and dancing on roller skates: "Can it be, I like myself? She likes me, so I like myself...") – although he is by no means fit for roller skating any longer and in ten years will be seventy-three and she will only by then be fifty-five so this prospect of love (perhaps extremely remote prospect of love is a more accurate term) seems doomed to fail (and there you have *that* again!), maybe has already failed, making him wonder if "love" is perhaps only a temporal thing (immortal love does seem a rather romance-comic-book romantic notion when it comes to the crunch of the cornflakes), and in truth what could she possibly see in him, he doesn't even like her to see his aging body naked although he does *extremely* enjoy seeing *her* in that state, trim and tanned and creamed and gleaming as her relatively young flesh is, *what an ass!* etc.

Is that what this is all about then, just lasciviousness? No, no, no, he has only seen her naked three times anyway (although his breath goes shallow remembering every detail of those three exhilarating experiences, nor does it have to do only with young flesh because Eileen was five years *older* than he and he was greatly enamored of her flesh even when it began to age and sag a bit, though he can't say how he might have felt if it had sagged a great deal more, but was spared that test by Eileen having ceased to love him when he still loved her), his primary pleasure has been taken far more from her (Lucia's) person, her manner, her words, than from her body (this went for both Eileen and for Lucia, although he cannot discount the piquancy of the fucking with Lucia – it was quite an experience for his sixty-three year old self to create the two-backed beast with Lucia's forty-five year old one – *wow, indeed* to put it mildly! – although he remembers meeting a woman of forty-five once when he was thirty-four and the two of them kissing, perhaps the nicest kisses he has ever experienced, her lips and mouth so knowing and engaged that he still recalls the kisses nearly thirty years later, although he also remembers thinking, from the vantage point of his thirties, how much older she seemed than he, while now he is thinking that forty-five is quite young indeed. Everything, it seems, is relative or even worse.

After his last physical meeting with Lucia, they sent lengthy e-mails to one another every day, filling the vast ether of their two-thousand-mile separation, sometimes twice a day, and every time he saw the name Lucia illuminated in his in-box, his heart leapt and his blood jumped, although he has to admit that then the e-mails began to come every other day, then twice a week, then once a week, and now he has not heard from her for fifteen days except for a couple of lines in which, however, she hastened to say she was *thinking* of him and which she signed "kisses" – though he is left in doubt as to whether she thought of those kisses in a literal sense or merely as a complimentary closing.

So, he thinks, what is he living off now? A word (kisses – an ambiguous word really) and the thought of his existing inside her pretty head (which might also be a hyperbole – what, after all, he thinks, does "*thinking* of you" really mean – thinking at the moment of writing those words or thinking more generally or even – do not rule this out – *wanting to tell him that she was thinking of him when in fact she was hardly thinking of him at all* or even thinking about how to extricate herself from this constant need to send him e-mails and from the prospect of having to be naked with him again?)

This is instructive, he thinks. This should be instructive. He thinks that he really should learn from this. What? he wonders. What should he learn? Perhaps, he thinks, this will finally teach him about the nature of love, the nature of loneliness, the nature of desire, the nature of life.

Don't be a fool, he thinks. Lucia is her own person and she owes him nothing at all and is free to decide against becoming involved with him and probably would be wise to do so because of the age difference and the geographical distance to name but two very salient matters.

Although he would prefer not to, he rises from the sofa, the slender book of poetry held open on his index finger, and pads across the carpet into his office to check his e-mail. There is no illuminated *Lucia* in his in-box so his blood does not jump but sinks with resignation.

Don't be a fool, he thinks. Who could blame her? A young beautiful woman like that has no need of an old fool like me. This was merely a flirtation. A fluttering of the pulses. A pleasant interlude. A temporary jumping of the blood through the fiery hoops. So let it rest.

He clicks the "refresh" tab on his screen. Two new e-mails appear, but neither is from Lucia, and the absence of Lucia's illuminated name in his inbox makes him feel incomplete, but he thinks that probably everyone always feels incomplete anyway, it being a condition of being alive to feel incomplete and particularly a condition of a man of his age who should not expect to be completed by a relatively much younger and still beautiful woman. That *is* it, and he realizes that he is to be spared the mysteries and surprises and disappointments and vicissitudes of this "love affair."

He closes the book which he was still holding open on his index finger at the poem whose first line had so beguiled him and returns it to its alphabetical slot on his poetry shelf under Rios, Alberto. Then he goes in to his office to shut down the laptop, but does look once more to see if the name Lucia is illuminated in the inbox, which it is not, and he cannot help but wonder what he would do if the name should suddenly appear on the screen, and she professed profound love for him – would he be glad or frightened? – or, conversely, continued to offer ambiguous statements, complimentary closings of "kisses" and "thinking of you" – and either way, it seems to him now, is a kind of potential fall, a gateway to a kind of Fall from Grace where a kind of spirit of frenzy lays in wait for him.

He remembers then that in one of her e-mails Lucia said something about having been "naked in his bed," and he remembers the details of her naked body – particularly perhaps her rump, how odd, he thinks again, to surrender one's heart to a rump, though other parts as well – and of Eileen's naked body and her rump, which he also cherished (definitely part of the chemistry: *My soul then sold for but a rump?/By those hips parenthesized?)* And he remembers once then in Dublin at a conference when he was rather loudly entertaining a group of colleagues in his hotel room late one night and stepped out into the hall to get more ice from the machine and a naked woman was standing outside the open door across the way, a most appealingly naked woman, and she spoke in fury to him, shouting, "Ye can shut the fuck up, ye can, all of ye!" and his mouth dropped open at the paradox of her inviting nakedness and her furious anger, and he muttered simply, "Yes, I will, of course, forgive me," and she disappeared into her room with a flash of comely rump, and now he returns to his poetry shelf to find the book he has just put back into its alphabetical slot and thumbs it open to the page and the line, "I am a slave to the nudity of women," and it occurs to him that that perhaps is all he knows and all he needs to know. But *he does not know with what resolve he could stand against it, a naked woman, asking of him anything.*

ABOUT THE AUTHOR

Thomas E. Kennedy's many books include novels, story and essay collections, literary criticism, anthologies, and translations. His stories, essays, poems, translations, and interviews appear regularly in American and European periodicals and anthologies and, among other awards, have won Pushcart and O. Henry prizes and a National Magazine Award. He is author of *The Copenhagen Quartet*, four independent novels about the seasons and souls of the Danish capital, the first volume of which, *In the Company of Angels*, was released by Bloomsbury in 2010, to be followed by the second in 2011. Kennedy's translation of Dan Turèll's *Last Walk Through the City* also appeared in 2010 as an illustrated bilingual edition.

Kennedy holds a B.A. from Fordham University Lincoln Center, an M.F.A. from Vermont College, and a Ph.D. from the University of Copenhagen and teaches in the Fairleigh Dickinson University low-residency M.F.A. program. He lives in Denmark where he is the father of a son, Daniel, and daughter, Isabel, and the mother-father of Leo Kennedy-Rye.

CPSIA information can be obtained at www.ICGtesting.com
Printed in the USA
LVOW120705191211

260076LV00001B/29/P

9 780981 780283